PEELING THE ORANGE

WHITE COLLAR CRIME TRIAL PROBLEM

SECOND EDITION

Lucian E. Dervan
Professor of Law and Director of Criminal Justice Studies
Belmont University College of Law

Ellen S. Podgor
Gary R. Trombley Family White-Collar Crime Research Professor
Professor of Law
Stetson University College of Law

CAROLINA ACADEMIC PRESS

Durham, North Carolina

ISBN: 978-1-5310-3384-2

Carolina Academic Press
700 Kent Street
Durham, North Carolina 27701
(919) 489-7486
www.cap-press.com

For Anne, who has made this and all my projects a reality.

LED

For Jake and Charlie Klausman.

ESP

Preface

Thank you for selecting *Peeling the Orange: White Collar Crime Trial Problem (2nd Ed.)*. In creating this complex hypothetical situation, we have drawn on our collective years in practice and the academy to create a realistic problem that introduces the reader to fundamental aspects of white collar criminal law and real-life practical challenges encountered by practitioners during these matters.

The book begins with a narrative description of the events at issue. This narrative takes the reader from the early moments of the alleged criminal scheme through the investigation and eventual prosecution of the matter. Along the way, the reader will see reference to documents that are contained in the second half of the book. These documents should be carefully examined in tandem with the narrative reading to present the most comprehensive, detailed, and realistic view of the case. These documents also reflect what an actual practitioner retained in this matter might encounter.

As would be true in a real case, this trial problem contains purposefully included errors, including errors in judgment by individuals, errors in the application of the law, and errors in the drafting of documents. These are inserted into the problem to challenge the reader to consider each action and document carefully. As you read the narrative and the attached documents, consider how you might have responded to the problems presented. Is this the decision you would have made in this situation? Can you challenge this document in court? Is this how you would have prepared this document? As the reader considers these questions, the reader should also think about the larger issues presented in this case regarding white collar crime and the complexities of this ever changing field of law.

Practitioners who have worked through this problem, some of whom are the leading white collar advocates in the country, have told us that this problem looks and feels like a real case with real world challenges and lessons. We hope you will enjoy this unique journey into the heart of a hypothetical white collar crime, investigation, and prosecution. Remember, fact is often stranger than fiction, especially in the world of white collar and corporate crime.

Note that the following format is used for years in the narrative and accompanying documents.

YEAR-0 – This represents the current year in which the trial and sentencing occur.
YEAR-1 – This represents the year before the trial and sentencing occur.
YEAR-2 – This represents the second year before the trial and sentencing occur, etc.

Lucian E. Dervan
Ellen S. Podgor
2026

Acknowledgements

Our sincerest thanks to all who have helped us in creating this problem, including our colleagues at Belmont University College of Law and Stetson University College of Law. Our thanks also to Belmont University College of Law and Stetson University College of Law for their support of our work.

Special thanks to Stetson University College of Law for their support of Stetson's White Collar Criminal Defense Training Program.

The authors also thank the following students from the White Collar Advocacy Class at Stetson University College of Law who contributed in the preparation of documents for this problem: Kate Susan Atkinson, Frank John Bane, Rachel Marie Batten, Adam Robert Bugg, Jamie Combee, Marisol Dusek Gomez, Daniel Scott Hartpence, Sabsina Nasim Karimi, Joshua Kohlman Luria, Andrew Dean Reder, Laura Anne Rose, Michael Anthony Scanio, Lauren Renee Senninger, Garrett Scott Severson, Walter Sowa, Jessie Marie Weissman, Amanda Marie Whitt, and others who have used prior versions of this advocacy problem. The authors also thank Stetson University College of Law faculty support, with special thanks to Shannon Edgar and Jessica Zook.

The authors also thank Henry W. Asbill for reading and commenting on the initial draft of this problem and those involved with Stetson's White Collar Criminal Defense Training Program for their helpful comments.

Table of Contents

PEELING THE ORANGE

WHITE COLLAR CRIME TRIAL PROBLEM

SECOND EDITION

I. Introduction to a White Collar Case

On October 12, YEAR-2, three employees of the Citrus Florida Community Company (CFC) gather in a conference room on the fourth floor of their corporate headquarters in Tampa, Florida. Present at the meeting are **Ashley Alden, Chris Smart,** and **Jess Henley**. CFC is a public company on the New York Stock Exchange. Alden heads CFC's product distribution division, a group charged with marketing and selling new products to CFC's existing customers. Smart and Henley work for Alden and each lead a team of twenty individuals. Smart's team works on marketing initiatives, and Henley's team works on sales.[1]

CFC was founded in 1895 as a small citrus processing entity. Over the decades, however, the company expanded into all areas of the citrus industry, including the production of their own orange juice brands, orange cleaning supply products, orange based air fresheners and other products with a citrus base. Currently, CFC distributes its materials to numerous national store chains and employs eight-thousand people. Many of CFC's employees work in processing plants scattered throughout the Southeast. In Georgia, for example, the company has a cleaning supply processing and packaging plant that employs six-hundred people. Products are shipped worldwide and CFC maintains a small two-person office in New York to handle the shipments made throughout the Northeast.

Approximately one-hundred and fifty people work at CFC's headquarters in Tampa, Florida, including the following:

Jody Murray – CEO and Chairperson of the Board of Directors
Kim Vanguard – Chief Operating Officer
Tracy Strain – Chief Financial Officer
Cory Campbell – General Counsel
Lynn Smith – Head of Corporate Compliance and Human Resources[2]

CFC also has a research and development (R&D) facility in Gulfport, Florida, approximately fifteen miles away from the Tampa headquarters. The facility is headed by **Dr. Sami Myers**, a researcher with over twenty-years of experience working in the citrus industry. The Gulfport R&D division headed by Dr. Myers contains fifty employees.

At the October 12, YEAR-2 meeting, Alden calls Dr. Myers on the telephone to discuss the test results for a new additive to orange juice called AOA. The additive is intended to achieve two results. First, it is thought the additive can prolong the length of time orange juice can remain on the shelf at retail establishments before it must be discarded. Second, it is thought that because the additive prolongs the length of time before the orange juice spoils, the orange juice will taste fresher than those from other producers. Because of this intended effect, CFC has ordered thousands of new orange juice containers that will include an "AOA" label and that will inform customers the label means the orange juice is fresher than competitors' brands. In fact, just two days before the call with Dr. Myers, Alden told investors and analysts during a conference call that preliminary test results looked very positive and that the new line of orange juice with the

[1] A Company Chart is included at the end with a Cast of Characters.
[2] Lynn Smith is not an attorney.

additive should hit the shelves in a couple of months. Alden also informed investors and analysts that because of the additive, CFC orange juice will sell for an additional dollar per liter, with half the increase being absorbed by retailers and the other half of the increase being passed along to consumers who choose to purchase orange juice with the "AOA" label.

Unfortunately, during the telephone conversation with Dr. Myers on October 12, YEAR-2, Alden, Smart, and Henley learn that the final test results now show the new additive is ineffective and the entire project must be scrapped.

"Wait a minute," says Alden. "You mean to tell me this whole project is a waste of time. I've got people on the street expecting this thing to hit the shelves any time now. What do you think is going to happen if they find out we've got nothing?"

"All I can tell you is the results," responds Dr. Myers. "The stuff just doesn't work."

"And who knows about these results?" asks Smart.

"I'm the only one who has looked at the issue really carefully," responds Dr. Myers.

Alden and Smart look at one another knowingly. "Ok then," says Alden. "Here is what's going to happen. You destroy those test results and we'll go ahead with the launch using the preliminary data. We'll just tell everyone the product works great."

"What do you mean?" asks Dr. Myers. "The product doesn't work. You're talking about falsifying test results and lying to retailers and consumers."

"That may be the case," barks Alden, "but we've got significant stock options that are about to vest, and I'm not about to let the street kill this stock right before I sell my shares."

"Fine," says Dr. Myers, "but I don't want anything to do with it. You say what you want, and I won't stop you. But I won't lie for you."

"That's good enough for me," responds Alden. "No one's going to ask you anyway. But make sure you destroy that data."

Alden hangs up on Dr. Myers and turns to Smart and Henley. "So, are we all in agreement about what needs to be done?" Both nod their head in agreement, though Henley is clearly apprehensive about what Alden and Smart have done. "Do you have a problem Henley," yells Alden.

"I'll follow your instructions Alden. You're the boss," responds Henley.

Unknown to Alden, Smart, or Henley, an employee, **Logan Walter**, who works for Smart on the marketing team is lingering in the hallway outside the conference room during this conversation. Walter can hardly believe what was said, but, not wanting to get in the middle of the situation, Logan Walter returns to their desk and continues their regular work.

Two weeks later, on October 26, YEAR-2, Alden announces at a press conference that the final test results show the AOA additive is effective and tells investors and analysts that seven national store chains have already made significant orders of the product. While it is true that seven national store chains have purchased the new orange juice, it was inaccurate to tell them that the final test results were positive.

In response to Alden's statements, CFC's stock increases from $28 a share to $34 a share. The next day, Alden and Smart execute their stock options and sell significant holdings of CFC stock. Alden makes $275,000 on the transaction, and Smart makes $120,000 on the transaction. Henley decides not to sell any stock as they still feel uncomfortable about what has been done. Dr. Myers keeps the sole copy of the final AOA test results locked in a filing cabinet, rather than destroying them as instructed by Alden. Though Dr. Myers is uncomfortable with the situation, they remain silent about the events and do not tell anyone that Alden was lying when it was stated that the test results were positive. The same day Alden and Smart sell their stock, Dr. Myers sells $55,000 in stock that had been received as stock options, making a profit of $25,000 on this sale.

In March YEAR-1, CFC's managers conduct their annual performance reviews of employees. Logan Walter has been experiencing difficulties at home and, as a result, has been underperforming at work. Smart completes Walter's performance review and rates Walter as "Below Expectations." When Walter sees this review, they become angry and decide that they won't remain silent any longer.

Walter marches upstairs to the fourth floor of the corporate headquarters and asks to speak with Lynn Smith, head of corporate compliance and human resources. Smith invites Walter into the office and asks Walter to describe what is concerning them. Walter then retells every detail of the telephone conversation that they overheard on October 12, Year-2. Throughout the interview, Smith takes extensive notes, including making comments about their impressions of Walter and the story being heard. Smith then decides to investigate the matter further. Smith interviews Alden, Smart, and Henley, again taking extensive notes each time. Each confirms the story told by Walter, but each argues they did what they thought was in the best interest of the company because they believed the additive would eventually be perfected and work as intended. Smith also interviews Dr. Myers, but Dr. Myers states that they disagreed with Alden's demands, but did not know what to do in response. This interview takes place in Dr. Myers' Gulfport office and, during the interview, Dr. Myers goes to the filing cabinet and retrieves the only copy of the final test results. Dr. Myers hands the results to Smith, who takes them back to their office. Smith does not ask questions regarding whether Alden, Smart, Henley, Walter, or Myers sold any of their stock during this period of time.

After completing this investigation, Smith puts together a file containing the interview notes and documents collected, including the final AOA test results. <u>See</u> Attachment A (Corporate Compliance Investigation File). Smith then takes the file to the office of the company's general counsel, Cory Campbell. Campbell reviews the file, does no additional investigation, and tells Smith to reprimand the employees in writing, but take no further action. This decision is driven by the fact that the AOA orange juice product was not profitable for the company. As a result, CFC stopped making the new orange juice two months after its launch. In Campbell's opinion, because the matter is behind the company and the product is no longer being offered to retailers or consumers, it is best to keep the matter internal to the company and not reveal the deceit to anyone else. Alden, Smart, and Henley are each to receive reprimand letters and their respective annual cash bonuses are reduced by 10%. This represents a punishment of $10,000, $5,000 and $5,000 respectively. Walter, the employee who complained to Smith, is informed that the matter is closed and that "appropriate action was taken against those who acted improperly." Walter is not told what was found during the investigation, who was punished as a result, or what punishment was delivered. Once the matter is closed, Smith sends the investigatory file back to Campbell for storage in the filing cabinet in the general counsel's office, with other files containing confidential legal material. Before placing the file in the cabinet, however, Campbell removes the final AOA test data document and shreds it.

By September YEAR-1, CFC has been hit hard by a cold freeze that destroys much of the orange crop in Florida. As a result, the company decides to perform a reduction in force. The process by which employees are selected for this reduction in force is by looking at their last performance review. Anyone who received a "Below Expectations" is placed on the list for termination. One of the two-hundred individuals on the list is Walter. When Walter receives their termination notice on October 1, YEAR-1, Walter becomes convinced that this termination is because of blowing the whistle on Alden, Smart, Henley, and Dr. Myers. As such, Walter hires an attorney who files a civil retaliation action against CFC, Alden, Smart, Henley, Dr. Myers and Smith on October 15, YEAR-1. The civil complaint includes specific discussion of the actions of Alden, Smart, Henley, and Dr. Myers in October YEAR-2. <u>See</u> Attachment B (Civil Complaint).

On October 20, YEAR-1 newspaper reporter Ali Angelo is checking on recent filings in the clerk's office and happens to find the civil complaint filed by Logan Walter. Ali Angelo writes an exposé in the local newspaper that describes what happened at CFC. <u>See</u> Attachment C (Newspaper Story). That day, CFC's stock drops from $30.00 to $5.00 per share with twenty-five million shares outstanding. The local United States Attorney for the Middle District of Florida reads the newspaper article and decides to ask someone to check out the civil complaint and its allegations. The matter is handed to Assistant United States Attorney **Jo Jones** and FBI Agent **Bernie Bentham**. At the same time, the Securities and Exchange Commission also launches an informal inquiry into the sale of stock by Alden, Smart, and Dr. Myers and the increase in CFC's stock price after the announcement of the launch of its new orange juice product in the fall of YEAR-2.

After interviewing Logan Walter, the AUSA, concerned about the destruction of possible evidence following the newspaper story, decides to execute a search warrant at CFC's headquarters in Tampa and its research facility in Gulfport. The AUSA drafts an affidavit to support its application for a warrant and presents it to a local magistrate judge. <u>See</u> Attachment D (Affidavit in Support of Warrant Application). The warrant is approved and, at 9:00 a.m. on November 1, YEAR-1, the FBI executes the search warrant. <u>See</u> Attachment E (Search Warrant).

II. <u>Retaining Counsel and Accompanying Ethical Issues</u>

Moments after the FBI arrives at CFC and begins executing the search warrant, Campbell calls the company's outside counsel. The lead attorney at the law firm is **Tomi Bell.**

"Tomi, it's Cory. We've got the FBI all over the building. I need you to come over here."

"Alright," responds Tomi Bell. "I'll be right there."

Later that day, Dr. Myers decides to retain counsel as a result of the FBI search. Sami Myers calls an attorney in Tampa who specializes in white collar criminal defense named **Dakota Holt**.

"Hello, this is Dr. Myers. I'm an employee at CFC. I'm sure you heard we were raided earlier today. I think I should come in and retain your services."

"Ok, let's have you come down right away," the attorney responds. "How about we meet in an hour?"

When Dr. Myers arrives, they bring along a copy of the corporate bylaws and their employment agreement. See Attachment F (Corporate Bylaws); Attachment G (Employment Agreement).

III. Handling the Search

A few days later, both Bell and Holt retrieve copies of the affidavit in support of the search warrant from the federal courthouse. When they read the affidavit, they each carefully review the document for the probable cause that justified the warrant. They also review the document with regard to the particularity of the place to be searched and the items to be seized, as required under the Fourth Amendment. Further, it has become evident since the search that the government seized an incredible volume of materials, including almost every document contained in the offices of Alden, Smart, Henley, and Dr. Myers. Further, the government seized the computers used by these employees. In the case of Dr. Myers, the government seized two laptop computers from their office. One was a company issued laptop, but the other was a personal laptop, which Dr. Myers sometimes brought into the office. Dr. Myers had some problems with the office laptop and occasionally used the personal laptop when conducting company business.

IV. Investigating the Case and Accompanying Ethical Issues

Following the return of items from the search, AUSA Jo Jones opens a grand jury investigation of CFC. The U.S. Food and Drug Administration (FDA) also begins an investigation of CFC.

After meeting with their respective client's, Bell and Holt decide to begin investigating the case. Bell informs the corporation of the need to have access to documents and employees. Bell then issues two memoranda to the employees on November 3, YEAR-1. The first memoranda instructs the employees to suspend all document destruction protocols. See Attachment H (CFC Document Retention Memoranda). The second memoranda instructs the employees to assist in the collection of documents and materials related to the subject of the government investigation. See Attachment I (CFC Document Search Memoranda).

Holt instructs Dr. Myers to come back to the office the next afternoon so they can discuss the case further.

During this internal corporate investigation, Bell schedules a meeting with Alden. Each of the employees involved in the investigation—along with the prominent officers and directors at the company—now have counsel, and Alden's counsel was informed of the scheduled interview. At the beginning of the meeting, Alden informs Bell that they will not answer any questions at that time. Rather, Alden tells Bell that they will need to get in touch with their counsel to discuss the details of any subsequent meeting. Bell then telephones Alden's counsel, who informs Bell that they would like to discuss a joint defense agreement before proceeding any further.

Bell then moves on to the scheduled meeting with Smart, whose counsel was also informed of the meeting. When Bell walks in to speak with Smart, Smart stands up and informs Bell that counsel said not to speak with any internal corporate counsel. Smart states, "I will not cooperate with the company's investigation in any way." Smart then leaves the room.

Bell, disappointed in not being able to meet with Alden or Smart, goes on to the next scheduled meeting with an employee working on the sales team under Henley. At the beginning of the meeting, the employee, named **Jamie Tate**, turns to Bell and asks, "Do you think I need an attorney?" Bell responds, "That's up to you," and then goes on with the interview. At the conclusion of the interview, Bell takes the handwritten notes from the meeting and uses them to construct an interview memorandum. See Attachment J (Interview Notes); Attachment K (Interview Memoranda). Bell then takes the handwritten interview notes and shreds them.

Later that day, Dr. Myers meets with attorney Dakota Holt. Myers brings to this meeting a large stack of documents.

"What are these?" asks Holt.

"Before I left work today, I grabbed a number of important documents about my research study into the orange juice additive. These are the originals from that entire process, excluding the final data results which I turned over to Smith."

V. Grand Jury Subpoenas

Four weeks later, AUSA Jones asks a grand jury investigating the case to issue subpoenas. The grand jury issues subpoenas for documents to the company on December 1, YEAR-1. See Attachment L (Grand Jury Subpoena). Included are broad requests that appear to cover matters well outside the orange juice additive investigation, including allegations of channel stuffing[3] of

[3] "Channel stuffing" is a term used to describe the act of pushing excess product, here orange juice, through distribution channels despite there being an inability to sell the excess product to the end customer. This practice is someone utilized by corporations to falsely inflate sales and profitability figures and/or inaccurately create the

products to retailers to meet quarterly sales goals. The requests also ask for extensive electronic materials, including the entire contents of certain employees' network drives—Smith, Alden, Smart, Henley, and Dr. Myers. The subpoena also asks for the calendars/diaries of each of these employees. Further, one request specifically covers any materials related to any internal investigation of the AOA additive matter conducted by the corporate compliance/human resources office. Attorney Tomi Bell approaches Lynn Smith, and is informed by Smith that the internal review file is being held by General Corporate Counsel Cory Campbell. When Bell visits with the General Counsel, Campbell tells Bell two things. First, Campbell claims that the file folder and its contents are covered by the attorney-client privilege and work product doctrines because Campbell reviewed the materials and advised Smith on how to proceed. Second, Campbell informs Bell of the destruction of the final test results for the additive after the internal investigation was concluded.

The grand jury also issues subpoenas for documents and testimony to Alden, Smart, Henley, and Dr. Myers on December 1, YEAR-1. See Attachment M (Grand Jury Subpoenas). Holt calls Dr. Myers into the office and informs Myers of the subpoena.

"How should I respond?" Myers asks. "I don't think I should even show up. I might say something that lands me in trouble. Isn't that what happened to Martha Stewart?"

Ashley Alden is particularly concerned about the request for their diary. Alden has been having an affair for the last year and is concerned that it will come to light if they see where they have spent time during the last year. Ashley Alden takes the diary and shreds it.

VI. Parallel Proceedings

On December 7, YEAR-1, one week after the grand jury subpoenas arrive, the company (CFC), Smith, Alden, Smart, Henley, and Dr. Myers receive requests for production in the civil retaliation case. The civil requests for production are extremely broad and request materials similar to those being sought by the government. See Attachment N (Request for Production in Civil Retaliation Case). The parties also receive requests to set depositions in the civil matter. See Attachment O (Request for Depositions in Civil Retaliation Case). Around the same time, the company also receives a request for documents from the Securities and Exchange Commission, the U.S. Attorney's Office in the Southern District of New York, and from the New York Attorney General's Office. See Attachment P (SEC Request for Documents); Attachment Q (U.S. Attorney's Office for the Southern District of New York Request for Documents); Attachment R (New York Attorney General's Office Request for Documents).

VII. Making Presentations to the Government & Proffers

Sensing the grand jury is wrapping up its investigation, both Bell and Holt contact the United States Attorney's Office and request they be permitted to come in to give presentations regarding why their clients should not be prosecuted. AUSA Jones agrees and each is given one

appearance a product is in high demand.

hour to convince the government that their client should not be indicted.

VIII. Plea Offers, Deferred Prosecution Agreements, and Non-Prosecution Agreements

Attorney Tomi Bell arrives at the meeting with the government with notebooks in hand, all neatly tabbed for easy use by the government. The contents of these notebooks include evidence that would be helpful to the government if they sought to prosecute Alden, Smart, Henley, Myers, or CEO Jody Murray. Included in these notebooks are statements of Cory Campbell and Lynn Smith regarding the conversations with company employees. Tomi Bell also included an email that Cory Campbell sent to CFC CEO Jody Murray following the meeting with Lynn Smith. In this email, Cory Campbell tells CEO Jody Murray about Lynn Smith's investigation. CEO Jody Murray responded to this email by thanking Cory Campbell for handling this situation. Murray says, "It's nice to know that you are my attorney." See Attachment S (Emails Between Cory Campbell and CEO Jody Murray). One of the emails states,

> We represent the company. These conversations are privileged, but the privilege belongs to the company and the company decides whether to waive it. If there is a conflict, the attorney-client privilege belongs to the company.

Also in the notebooks are copies of the awards and bonuses that CEO Jody Murray gave to Alden, Smart, and Henly for their loyalty to CFC. See Attachment T (Copies of the Award Certificates and Bonuses). Attorney Tomi Bell uses the materials in these notebooks to try and convince the government not to prosecute the company. AUSA Jo Jones offers a deferred prosecution agreement to CFC. See Attachment U (Deferred Prosecution Agreement Offered to CFC).

Holt also explores with AUSA Jo Jones a possible plea agreement for Myers. Jones offers a plea to Myers to plead to one count of mail fraud with no stipulation as to the sentence to be received. The plea agreement requires Myers to waive all appellate rights and all discovery rights including the right to receive *Brady* material. The plea also requires Myers to agree to waive any right to later claim that Holt was ineffective. See Attachment V (Plea Agreement Offered to Myers). AUSA Jo Jones tells Holt that if Myers fails to accept the plea within the next 24 hours, an indictment will be forthcoming.

IX. Client Charged and Bail

CFC accepts the deferred prosecution agreement offered by the government and turns over materials to AUSA Jones that will assist in the prosecution of CEO Murray, Campbell, Alden, Smart, Henley, and Myers. Within hours of reaching this agreement, CFC is flooded with shareholder lawsuits and a new request for discovery from Logan Walter. Walter's civil discovery request seeks to obtain copies of all materials turned over to the government. The argument is made that the release of these materials to the government waives any possible attorney-client privilege that might have previously existed with respect to the contents of the materials in the hands of Campbell and Bell.

Myers, however, decides not to accept the plea that was offered.

The government is aware that Murray, Myers, Henley, and Smart all have children attending the ABC Elementary School, a local private school, and that parent-teacher night is the next evening. At 8 p.m. on December 16, YEAR-1, five vehicles with FBI vested individuals arrive at the school. They enter the school in the middle of the open house and arrest Murray, Myers, Henley, and Smart. They handcuff each of them and walk them out of the building to the awaiting federal vehicles. The media, tipped off about this arrest, are busy snapping pictures of Murray, Myers, Henley, and Smart as they exit the building in handcuffs and enter into the awaiting vehicles. Myers calls Holt from the booking office.

Newspaper reporter Ali Angelo writes a story in the local paper about the arrest. The story contains information that could only have been obtained from someone in the grand jury room. The newspaper article states that it received information from a high ranking government official.

CEO Murray and GC Campbell are charged with wire fraud under the honest services provision. Campbell is also charged with obstruction of justice. Myers, Henley, Alden, and Smart are charged with mail fraud (honest services), securities fraud, insider trading, and conspiracy to commit mail fraud (honest services). Alden also receives a charge of obstruction of justice for shredding the diary. See Attachment W (Indictment of Murray, Campbell, Myers, Henley, Alden, and Smart).

X. Trial Preparation, Hiring Experts, and Discovery

Attorneys for Murray, Campbell, Myers, Henley, Alden and Smart enter into a joint defense agreement. See Attachment X (Joint Defense Agreement). Each of the parties files a request to the government to obtain discovery. See Attachment Y (Discovery Motion). The government sends a notice to counsel that all documents are located in a room at 15 Main Street, Sarasota and that they may view all documents there. The room does not contain a photocopy machine and to obtain copies of any documents, it is necessary for counsel to give the document to a government agent who will photocopy it for counsel. Counsel is instructed that no documents may be removed from the room. The documents are all printed on paper and there is no searchable method for viewing the documents, despite the fact that the government has everything in their offices on searchable CDs.

The defense group decides to hire two experts. First, they hire a forensic accountant, **Mickey Miller**, who is tasked with determining if there are any losses to anyone should the government be successful in proving its case. Miller is also asked to provide for each individual defendant an assessment of their fraud loss. Miller is a forensic accountant that routinely prepares cases for defense counsel and Dakota Holt, Myer's attorney, had previously used Miller in past cases. See Attachment Z (Letter Hiring Mickey Miller).

Second, the defense group hires a professor from Cal Tech, **Amari Andersen**, who has done extensive studies in extending the longevity in liquid products. See Attachment AA (Letter Hiring Amari Andersen).

XI. Pre-trial Motions, Jury Selection, Opening Statements, and New Discovery

Despite continual prodding, Jo Jones has not been particularly forthcoming in providing discovery and has not given the defense any Jencks material, even though the case is set for trial in three days. On the Friday before the start of Monday's trial, a package arrives to each of defense counsel's offices. Contained within the package are FBI 302s. See Attachment BB (FBI 302s). Despite the fact that some of the material is exculpatory to the defense, it is first provided to them on the Friday prior to the start of a Monday trial. This is also the first time that defense counsel is apprised of the fact that the government wiretapped Ashley Alden's telephone. There are 20 hours of tapes that arrive to each of defense counsel that Friday afternoon and the tapes include some exculpatory material for each of the defendants.

Ashley Alden is now deeply concerned as the tapes include conversations between Ashley and their lover. With the indictment, Ashley's marriage had been tenuous this past year, and Ashley is concerned that if the tapes are played at trial it will be the end of this marriage. On the eve of trial, Ashley Alden decides to accept a government plea to one count of securities fraud. The agreement requires Alden to provide truthful testimony at trial against the co-defendants. The agreement does not say anything about the government filing a 5K1.1 motion at sentencing. See Attachment CC (Ashley Alden's Plea Agreement).

Dakota Holt files a Motion in Limine on the morning of trial asking that certain statements of Alden's be precluded from being admitted because they contain bolstering hearsay evidence. Specifically requested are statements regarding what Alden told their lover and spouse about what Myers stated with regard to the worthlessness of AOA in providing longevity to the shelf life of orange juice. **Judge Jordan Justice** grants this motion and instructs prosecutors that they are not to reference these conversations unless the door is opened by the defense and only after a bench conference in which the court agrees that the door has been opened by defense counsel. Despite Judge Justice's grant of this motion in limine, Jo Jones states in opening statement the following, "You will hear tapes in which Ashley Alden is telling their spouse what Myers said – they said, the OJ AOA does not work." Dakota Holt jumps up, approaches the bench, and objects to this testimony. Judge Justice is annoyed by Jo Jones' deliberate violation of the court's order and grants the motion to strike and admonishes the jury to disregard what Jones just stated.

XII. Cross Examination of Government Witnesses

The government presents several witnesses including a government expert on the worthlessness of "AOA" and how Myers did not use accepted scientific measures in testing. See Attachment DD (Grand Jury Testimony of Government Witness Lee Laser). Laser's testimony is directly contrary to what the defense learned from their own expert witness, Cal Tech Professor Amari Andersen. See Attachment EE (Report of Defense Witness Professor Amari Andersen). In Laser's testimony to the jury there is a mention of a report that was prepared for the government. This report was never provided to defense counsel. Additionally, Laser's direct examination testimony differs somewhat from what Laser presented to the grand jury. See Attachment FF (Direct Examination of Lee Laser).

Alden takes the witness stand on behalf of the government. Alden states that it was Smart and Henley that convinced Alden to disregard the findings of Myers and proceed with announcing the new product. Alden also states that they were receiving pressure from CEO Jody Murray to increase sales and that they received bonuses from Murray based upon the increases in sales. Alden states, "Of course Jody Murray knew what was going on." See Attachment GG (Direct Examination of Ashley Alden).

The government uses FBI Agent Bernie Bentham to admit the tape recordings from the wire on Alden's telephone. Despite the court's order on the motion in limine, Jo Jones did not redact the recordings and the jury listens to conversations that contain statements between Alden and their spouse regarding what Myers allegedly stated. Judge Justice is irate on hearing this and asks counsel to approach the bench. While at the bench, the portion of the testimony containing the inadmissible evidence is left on the screen for the jury to read. Judge Justice asks Dakota Holt if there is any motion that they would like to make. Dakota Holt hesitates and in addition to objecting to the admission of this testimony, also moves for a mistrial.

XIII. Direct Examination

Judge Justice denies the defense motion for a mistrial and also denies the defense motion for acquittal. Dakota Holt and other counsel struggle with whether they should present any defense as the government's case was extraordinarily weak. The government has not presented any direct evidence regarding Myer's *mens rea*. Myers told counsel that the reason the stock was sold at that time was because their son was about to go off to college and they were selling the stock to pay the tuition. After discussion, it is determined that they would only present Professor Amari Andersen. Professor Andersen tells of the wonderful scientific work conducted by Myers. Andersen states that the test results failed to show how successful the product really could be. Andersen states that the real problem was with the test and not with the final product. Had the test been conducted in a slightly different fashion, it would have demonstrated that Myers was, in fact, correct in the initial assessment of "AOA" producing longevity in citrus products.

CEO Jody Murray wants very much to take the witness stand but counsel tells Murray not to take the risk. Counsel says "You have a good chance in winning it as it now stands, I think we should just rest." With that, the defense rests, reaffirming their motion for acquittal.

XIV. Jury Instructions and Closing Argument

Judge Justice says that they intend to use the standard jury instructions of the 11th Circuit. AUSA Jo Jones requests a specific instruction on willful blindness be given for Jodi Murray and Sami Myers. See Attachment HH (Government's Proposed Jury Instruction on Willful Blindness). Counsel for Murray and Myers vehemently object. They argue alternatively that if an instruction is given, that it reflect recent Supreme Court jurisprudence on this subject.

The court denies the defense motion requesting that a willful blindness instruction not be given, but then accepts the defense proposed jury instruction on willful blindness. See Attachment II (Defense and Court Instruction on Willful Blindness). The court's other instructions include an honest services instruction, reasonable and good faith defense, and definition of knowing and willfulness. See Attachment JJ (Honest Services Instruction, Reasonable and Good faith Defense, and Definition of Knowing and Willfulness). The parties then present closing arguments.

XV. Sentencing, Prison Preparation, and Collateral Consequences

Murray and Henley are acquitted of all charges. Myers and Smart, however, are each convicted of one count of securities fraud and Campbell is convicted of one count of honest services mail fraud. The court sets the matter for sentencing. Mickey Miller works with counsel for Myers and Smart in determining whether there is a fraud loss and how much it might be. Judge Justice has sent a copy of the jury verdict to the disciplinary board in Campbell's home state and they are calling for an immediate disbarment of Campbell's law license.

CAST OF CHARACTERS

The Corporation

Citrus Florida Community Company (CFC) (Tampa, Florida)
(8,000 employees)

Jody Murray (CEO and Chairperson of the Board of Directors)

Kim Vanguard
(Chief Operating Officer)

Tracy Strain
(Chief Financial Officer)

Cory Campbell
(General Counsel)

Lynn Smith
(Head of Corporate Compliance)

Ashley Alden
(Head, Product Distribution Div.)
(42 employees)

Dr. Sami Myers
(Head, CFC Research Facility)
(Gulfport, Florida) (50 employees)

Chris Smart
(Head, Marketing Team)
(20 employees)

Jess Henley
(Head, Sales Team)
(20 employees)

Logan Walter
(Member, Marketing Team)

Jamie Tate
(Member, Sales Team)

CAST OF CHARACTERS

Government Agents

Jo Jones (Assistant United States Attorney, Middle District of Florida)

Bernie Bentham (FBI Agent)

Outside Counsel

Tomi Bell (Counsel for the Corporation)

Dakota Holt (Counsel for Dr. Meyers)

Jan Smartz (Counsel for Logan Walter's)

Judge

Jordan Justice

Newspaper Reporter

Ali Angelo

Defense Experts

Mickey Miller (Forensic Accountant)

Amari Andersen (Cal Tech Professor)

Government Experts

Lee Laser (Professor)

TRIAL PROBLEM EXHIBITS

Trial Problem Exhibits Index

Attachment A	Corporate Compliance Investigation File Prepared and Assembled by Lynn Smith (includes interview notes from speaking with Walter Logan, Ashley Alden, Chris Smart, Jess Henley, and Dr. Sami Myers; it also includes a list of documents that had been in the file, which included the AOA test results prior to Cory Campbell shredding them)
Attachment B	Civil Complaint Filed by Logan Walter
Attachment C	Newspaper Story Written by Ali Angelo Describing the Contents of the Complaint Filed by Logan Walter
Attachment D	Affidavit in Support of Warrant Application Attachment
Attachment E	Search Warrant for Tampa and Gulfport Offices
Attachment F	Corporate Bylaws and Applicable Statute re Indemnification
Attachment G	Employment Agreement between Dr. Sami Myers and CFC
Attachment H	CFC Document Retention Memoranda
Attachment I	CFC Document Search Memoranda
Attachment J	Interview Notes Taken by Tomi Bell of the Interview with Jamie Tate
Attachment K	Interview Memoranda Prepared by Tomi Bell from the Notes of the Interview with Jamie Tate
Attachment L	Grand Jury Subpoena for Documents from CFC
Attachment M	Grand Jury Subpoenas for Documents and Testimony to Alden, Smart, Henley, and Dr. Myers
Attachment N	Request for Production in Civil Retaliation Case
Attachment O	Request for Depositions in Civil Retaliation Case
Attachment P	SEC Request for Documents
Attachment Q	U.S. Attorney's Office for the Southern District of New York Request for Documents
Attachment R	New York Attorney General's Office Request for Documents
Attachment S	Emails between Cory Campbell and CEO Jody Murray

Attachment T	Copies of the Awards and Bonuses that CEO Jody Murray Gave to Alden, Smart, and Henley for Their Loyalty to CFC
Attachment U	Deferred Prosecution Agreement Offered to CFC
Attachment V	Plea Agreement Offered to Myers
Attachment W	Indictment of Murray, Campbell, Myers, Henley, Alden, and Smart
Attachment X	Joint Defense Agreement
Attachment Y	Discovery Motion
Attachment Z	Letter Hiring Mickey Miller
Attachment AA	Letter Hiring Amari Andersen
Attachment BB	FBI 302s
Attachment CC	Ashley Alden's Plea Agreement
Attachment DD	Grand Jury Testimony of Government Witness Lee Laser
Attachment EE	Report of Defense Witness Professor Amari Andersen
Attachment FF	Direct Examination of Lee Laser
Attachment GG	Direct Examination of Ashley Alden
Attachment HH	Government's Proposed Jury Instruction on Willful Blindness
Attachment II	Defense and Court Instruction on Willful Blindness
Attachment JJ	Honest Services Instruction, Reasonable and Good Faith Defense, and Definition of Knowing and Willfulness

CFC Corporate Compliance Investigation File

Matter – CC-01234-05 re CFC AOA Additive

Index

Attachment A

Lynn Smith's Interview Notes – Interview of Logan Walter (March 23, YEAR-1)

- Walter works on the Marketing Team.
    - Reports to Chris Smart – Head of Marketing Team.
- Wants to report potential misconduct by Chris Smart (note timing – just after performance reviews issued).
- Allegation – Overheard something being discussed by Smart in late YEAR-2. Jess Henley and Ashley Alden were also in the room during the discussion. Notes there was someone on the telephone as well, but unsure who. Walter in the hallway the entire time. Doesn't think they knew they were there.
    - Group discussing the AOA orange juice additive.
    - Discussed the results of some testing regarding the impact of AOA on shelf life and freshness.
    - Walter says the person on the telephone said the product didn't work. Alden flipped out – began yelling at the person on the telephone.
        - Note to self – Late YEAR-2was around the time of the AOA launch. Look into timing of alleged conversation related to launch announcement.
    - Alden told the person on the telephone to destroy the test results and pretend the product worked. The person on the telephone agreed.
    - Smart agreed to help Alden right away. Henley was reluctant, but after Alden yelled at Henley, Henley agreed to follow Alden's instructions.
- Why brining this forward now?
    - Walter alleges they wanted to come forward earlier, but thought they might be punished in retaliation. No support for this allegation.
    - Asked Walter if any disagreements with Smart recently. Said no.
- Anything else I need to know?
    - No.
- Need to call Cory regarding this issue. What are the legal implications of saying a product does something it does not? What is the potential exposure in this case?
- Check Code of Conduct issues.

Future Interview Plan:
Alden
Smart
Henley
Myers
?

Attachment A

Lynn Smith's Interview Notes – Interview of Ashley Alden (March 23, YEAR-1)

- Alden – Head of Product Distribution Division.
  - Reports to Kim Vanguard (COO)
  - Leads Marketing Team (Chris Smart) and Sales Team (Jess Henley)
- Alden recalls the AOA program:
  - Excellent product potential. Recalls the excitement regarding the product when it was announced that initial testing was positive. "I thought I was going to retire on this thing."
  - Recalls that final testing was underway in the fall of YEAR-2.
- Final Test Results:
  - Informed Alden I was investigating the final test results and what they said about the product's effectiveness. Alden responded by saying nothing for a minute. Looked uneasy. Then responded, "I did it for the company. That was a good product. I don't care what those results said. With a little more work, AOA would have done what we promised. No question."
  - I asked Alden to explain. Responded that in October of YEAR-2 the final test results were due to be completed. Just before Alden had told investors and analysts that the product was great and that it would be rolled out shortly in new containers. "The market was hot for the product."
  - But the results that came back from Dr. Sami Myers (Head, CFC Research Facility, Gulfport) were bad. Myers said we couldn't show any positive impact from the AOA. It meant the whole thing was a "waste."
  - So they told Myers to forget the new test results. Just go with the preliminary results instead. "We knew with a little more work AOA would work, but we couldn't afford to wait any longer. We had to launch." People in the company expected action, not more sitting around. "We needed to increase sales."
    - CFC would never have hit the quarter without that launch.
    - Pre-ordered the containers with the AOA stamp.
  - Learned about test results on conference call. Chris Smart (Head, Marketing Team) and Jess Henley (Head, Sales Team) were in the room. Dr. Myers was on the telephone. No one else present.
  - Can't remember what anyone said specifically. Recalls that everyone was in agreement that the product needed to be launched regardless of the test results.
  - Destroying test results? Alden doesn't remember what Alden said, except remembers being furious.
    - Where are test results now? Doesn't know. Doesn't have copy. Never had copy of the test results.
    - Alden's temper showing. Heard about this before. Check YEAR-12 compliance files for investigation re harassment.
  - Any notes from that meeting? No.
  - Press conference launching the product? What was said?
    - Alden doesn't remember specifically. Can't recall if said anything specific about the test results. Felt confident it would work eventually, so didn't see anything wrong with going forward with the launch. Good for company.

Attachment A

        - Alden remembers discussing the orders that national stores had already placed for the new product.
    - Product discontinued after about two months because no profit. Thought this was all behind them. Asked why it was coming back now. Said there had been a complaint filed about the issue. Wouldn't reveal the ID of the person who reported.
        - Told Alden no retaliate if find out who made the report. Informed regarding Code of Conduct requirements re retaliation. Alden agreed.
- Anything else I need to know?
    - Alden said no.

Attachment A

Lynn Smith's Interview Notes – Interview of Chris Smart (March 23, YEAR-1)

- Smart – Head of Marketing Team
  - Reports to Ashley Alden (Head, Product Distribution Division)
  - Leads a team of twenty (note, Logan Walter is on Smart's team)
- Smart recalls AOA program:
  - Mentioned it was brilliant marketing idea.
  - Sorry it didn't turn out to be profitable for the company.
- Final Test Results:
  - Informed Smart I was investigating the final test results and what they said about the product. Smart asked if I'd spoken to Alden. Told Smart I would speak to everyone involved in the AOA product launch. Smart asked what I was interested in regarding the AOA additive. Told them I was informed the final test results showed the product didn't work but it was launched in any case.
  - Smart responded, "Yes. But it was the only option."
    - Alleged company had so much money in the project it would have been irresponsible not to roll out the new packaging on time – "no matter what the test results said or didn't say."
    - Stated that the product was very close to working when these results came back. Felt confident it would work shortly after launch.
  - Remembers early test results were positive. Alden in charge of publicity initially. Smart was putting together some big ad buys for when the product was officially launched.
  - Meeting with Alden, Jess Henley (Head, Sales Team), and Dr. Sami Myers (Head, CFC Research Facility) to go over the final numbers. Late fall – maybe October. No one else present. Supposed to be cut and dry – quick meeting. But the numbers were bad.
    - Alden has temper. Got mad at Myers.
    - Alden told Myers to get rid of the new numbers and rely on the preliminary test results instead.
    - Myers didn't seem happy, but Myers agreed. Henley also. It was the only option. The company needed that product and we already had it ready to launch. People expected it to happen. People needed it to hit the numbers.
    - Did Alden specifically tell Myers to destroy the test results? Can't remember exactly what was said about the test results.
      - Seems to be lying. Shady.
    - Were the test results destroyed? Not sure. Never seen them. Doesn't know where they are now.
    - Any notes taken during the meeting? No. Anyone else taking notes? Not that Smart recalls.
  - Recalls launch of the product. Believes there were several major stores already signed up for the product by that point. Can't recall what, if anything, was said at the launch about the final test numbers.
- Anything else I need to know?
  - Smart said no.

Attachment A

Lynn Smith's Interview Notes – Interview of Jess Henley (March 23, YEAR-1)

- Henley – Head of Sales Team
    - Reports to Ashley Alden (Head, Product Distribution Division)
    - Leads a team of twenty
- Henley recalls AOA program:
    - Big program. Lots of meetings and time spent preparing for the launch.
- Final Test Results:
    - Informed Henley I was investigating the final test results and what they said about the product. Henley look very uncomfortable. Asked what specifically. Informed Henley I was told there were negative test results that were ignored. Henley said yes, but claimed it was Alden's idea.
        - Henley doesn't seem like the leader type. Seems like a follower.
    - Recalls preparing for the launch. Early test results were positive and Alden and Chris Smart (Head, Marketing Team) were gearing up for the big push. Henley was also preparing and getting ready for the sales team to push the new product with the AOA stamp on the customers.
    - Meeting with Alden, Smart, and Dr. Sami Myers (Head, CFC Research Facility) to go over the final numbers. Early October YEAR-2. No one else present. Myers was on the telephone.
        - Myers told us the test results were negative. No impact. No claim to additional shelf life or fresher taste. It meant the program was over.
            - "In a way, I was relieved the whole thing was going to be over."
        - But Alden wasn't someone you wanted to tell bad news. "I remember looking across the table at Alden and Alden was turning red. Alden was about to burst with anger." Alden told Myers to destroy the test results. But Myers was reluctant. In the end, Myers agreed. "We all agreed. It was Alden. You do what Alden tells you or you find another job."
        - We went ahead with the launch.
    - Product Launch:
        - When the product was officially launched shortly after this meeting, Henley was very uncomfortable. Recalls Alden telling the press the final test results showed AOA was effective and that a number of national store chains had already purchased the new orange juice.
            - "The part about the national store chains was true. The rest, well, I think you know." Didn't expect Alden to specifically mention anything about test results.
        - "All I cared about was not losing my job." Wasn't Henley's idea, but Henley went along with what Alden and Smart wanted to do. Kept quiet.
        - Used to have sleepless nights until the product got pulled because it was not profitable. That was the best thing that could have happened. It put everything behind Henley – until now.
- Anything else I need to know?
    - Henley said no.

Attachment A

Lynn Smith's Interview Notes – Interview of Dr. Sami Myers (March 23, YEAR-1)

- Myers – Head of CFC Research Facility (Gulfport, Florida).
  - Reports to Kim Vanguard (COO).
  - Leads a team of fifty employees.
  - Has over twenty years of experience in citrus industry.
- Myers recalls AOA program:
  - "I knew this would come back to get us eventually. I told Alden, but Alden wouldn't listen."
  - The product had been tested early on and showed signs of promise. Alden made some comments to investors and analysts as a result. Myers knew it was too early to say anything for sure.
  - Then the final testing came back and the numbers showed it was ineffective.
- Final Test Results:
  - Alden had scheduled a conference call to discuss the final test results. Myers recalls that they were on the telephone from their office in Gulfport. In the Tampa office it was Alden, Chris Smart (Head, Marketing Team), and Jess Henley (Head, Sales Team). No one else present as far as Myers knew.
  - Alden seemed excited to get started. Alden planned a big launch for later that week. When Myers told Alden the bad news, Alden got irate. "Alden could be nasty when the news was bad."
  - Alden was yelling and demanded that Myers destroy all the test evidence and results. Myers told Alden that they didn't want anything to do with the plan. But Myers did agree to keep quiet about the whole mess. "I recall Alden said, 'Just destroy those documents,' and slammed down the telephone." Myers was shocked.
  - Where are the final test results now? Myers retrieved a copy from a locked filing cabinet. Alleges this is the only remaining copy of the final test results. All other copies, including electronic copies, destroyed. "I didn't think it was right to destroy the final copy of the test results. No matter what Alden demanded of me."
    - Note: The test results provided by Myers were placed in the corporate compliance investigation file.
  - Any notes from that meeting? No.
- Anything else I need to know?
  - Myers said no.

Attachment A

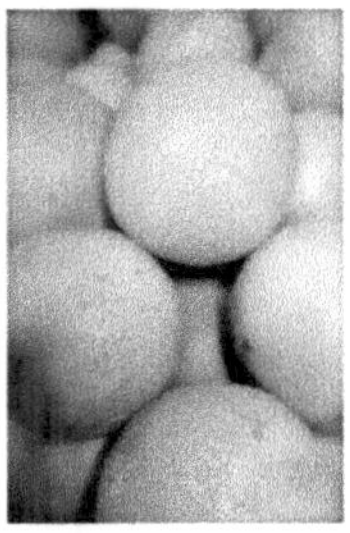

Citrus Florida Community Company
Since 1895

Lynn Smith
Head, Corporate Compliance
Citrus Florida Community
Company, Tampa, Florida

April 8, YEAR-1

Ashley Alden
Head, Product Distribution Division
Citrus Florida Community Company
Tampa, Florida

Re: *Corporate Compliance Investigation CC-01234-05*

Dear Alden:

As you are aware, the Citrus Florida Community Company has been conducting an internal review regarding the launch of the AOA juice additive. The investigation is now complete and a determination has been made that certain of your conduct violated the Citrus Florida Community Company's Corporate Code of Conduct. As a result, this letter of reprimand will be placed in your permanent Human Resources employment file. Further, your annual bonus for this fiscal year will be reduced by 10%.

Should you have any questions, please feel free to contact me.

Sincerely,

Lynn Smith
Head, Corporate Compliance

cc: Cory Campbell (General Counsel, Citrus Florida Community Company)

Attachment A

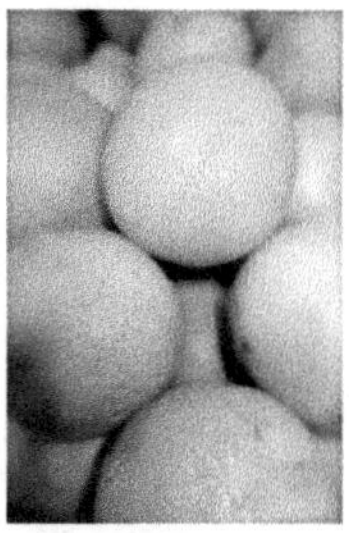

Citrus Florida Community Company
Since 1895

Lynn Smith
Head, Corporate Compliance
Citrus Florida Community
Company, Tampa, Florida

April 8, YEAR-1

Chris Smart
Head, Marketing Team
Citrus Florida
Community Company
Tampa, Florida

Re: *Corporate Compliance Investigation CC-01234-05*

Dear Smart:

As you are aware, the Citrus Florida Community Company has been conducting an internal review regarding the launch of the AOA juice additive. The investigation is now complete and a determination has been made that certain of your conduct violated the Citrus Florida Community Company's Corporate Code of Conduct. As a result, this letter of reprimand will be placed in your permanent Human Resources employment file. Further, your annual bonus for this fiscal year will be reduced by 10%.

Should you have any questions, please feel free to contact me.

Sincerely,

Lynn Smith
Head, Corporate Compliance

cc: Cory Campbell (General Counsel, Citrus Florida Community Company)

Attachment A

Citrus Florida Community Company
Since 1895

Lynn Smith
Head, Corporate Compliance
Citrus Florida Community
Company, Tampa, Florida

April 8, YEAR-1

Jess Henley
Head, Sales Team
Citrus Florida Community Company
Tampa, Florida

Re: *Corporate Compliance Investigation CC-01234-05*

Dear Henley:

As you are aware, the Citrus Florida Community Company has been conducting an internal review regarding the launch of the AOA juice additive. The investigation is now complete and a determination has been made that certain of your conduct violated the Citrus Florida Community Company's Corporate Code of Conduct. As a result, this letter of reprimand will be placed in your permanent Human Resources employment file. Further, your annual bonus for this fiscal year will be reduced by 10%.

Should you have any questions, please feel free to contact me.

Sincerely,

Lynn Smith
Head, Corporate Compliance

cc: Cory Campbell (General Counsel, Citrus Florida Community Company)

Attachment A

Citrus Florida Community Company
Since 1895

Lynn Smith
Head, Corporate Compliance
Citrus Florida Community
Company, Tampa, Florida

April 8, YEAR-1

Dr. Sami Myers
Head, CFC Research Facility
Citrus Florida Community
Company Gulf Port, Florida

Re: *Corporate Compliance Investigation CC-01234-05*

Dear Dr. Myers:

As you are aware, the Citrus Florida Community Company has been conducting an internal review regarding the launch of the AOA juice additive. The investigation is now complete and a determination has been made that certain of your conduct violated the Citrus Florida Community Company's Corporate Code of Conduct. As a result, this letter of reprimand will be placed in your permanent Human Resources employment file. Further, your annual bonus for this fiscal year will be reduced by 10%.

Should you have any questions, please feel free to contact me.

Sincerely,

Lynn Smith
Head, Corporate Compliance

cc: Cory Campbell (General Counsel, Citrus Florida Community Company)

Attachment A

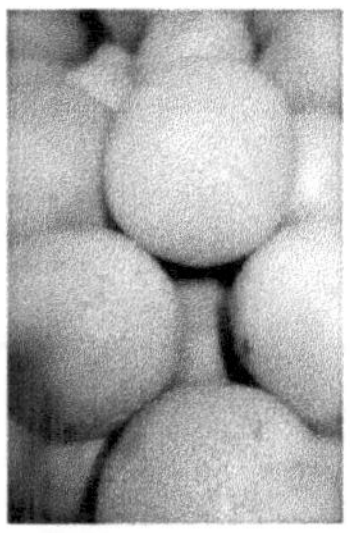

Citrus Florida Community Company
Since 1895

Lynn Smith
Head, Corporate Compliance
Citrus Florida Community
Company, Tampa, Florida

April 8, YEAR-1

Logan Walter
Marketing Team
Citrus Florida Community Company
Tampa, Florida

Re: *Corporate Compliance*

Dear Walter:

Thank you again for bringing your concerns to me regarding the launch of the AOA juice additive. A thorough investigation of the matter has now been concluded and appropriate action was taken regarding those who acted improperly.

Should you have any questions, please feel free to contact me.

Sincerely,

Lynn Smith
Head, Corporate Compliance

cc: Cory Campbell (General Counsel, Citrus Florida Community Company)

Attachment A

STATE OF FLORIDA
IN THE CIRCUIT COURT FOR THE THIRTEENTH JUDICIAL CIRCUIT
IN AND FOR HILLSBOROUGH COUNTY, FLORIDA

LOGAN WALTER)
)
Plaintiff,)
)
vs.)
)
CITRUS FLORIDA COMMUNITY COMPANY,)
a Florida Corporation, ASHLEY ALDEN, CHRIS)
SMART, JESS HENLEY, SAMI MYERS, and)
LYNN SMITH)
)
Defendants.)
_______________________________________)

COMPLAINT AND DEMAND FOR JURY TRIAL

1. Plaintiff, LOGAN WALTER, by and through undersigned counsel, hereby sues Defendants, CITRUS FLORIDA COMMUNITY COMPANY (hereinafter "CFC"), a Florida Corporation, ASHLEY ALDEN, CHRIS SMART, JESS HENLEY, SAMI MYERS, and LYNN SMITH.

INTRODUCTION

2. This action is brought by WALTER, a former CFC employee, and alleges a claim for violation of Florida's Private Sector Whistle Blower Act, sections 448.101 *et seq.*, Florida Statutes (hereinafter, the "Private Whistle Blower Act").

JURISDICTION, VENUE AND PARTIES

3. The claim herein is for damages in excess of $15,000.00, and this Court therefore has original, exclusive jurisdiction pursuant to section 26.012(2), Florida Statutes. Jurisdiction also arises, in part, under the Private Whistleblower Act.

Attachment B

4. At all times material to this complaint, Plaintiff WALTER was a resident of Hillsborough County, Florida and employed by CFC in the marketing division until they were terminated on October 1, YEAR-1.

5. CFC is a Florida Corporation that produces orange juice and other citrus based products and has its principal place of business in Hillsborough County, Florida.

6. Ashley Alden is a resident of Hillsborough County, Florida. Alden was at all times material to this complaint the head of CFC's product distribution division.

7. Chris Smart is a resident of Hillsborough County, Florida. Smart was at all times material to this complaint the head of CFC's marketing division and Plaintiff WALTER'S direct supervisor.

8. Jess Henley is a resident of Hillsborough County, Florida. Henley was at all times material to this complaint the head of CFC's product sales division.

9. Sami Myers is a resident of Hillsborough County, Florida. Myers was at all times material to this complaint the head of CFC's Gulfport research facility.

10. Lynn Smith is a resident of Hillsborough County, Florida. Smith was at all times material to this complaint the head of CFC corporate compliance and human resources.

11. Jurisdiction is proper pursuant to section 47.051, Florida Statutes, as this case is brought in the county where the cause of action accrued and where the Defendant Corporation conducts business and has its principal place of business and where the remaining defendants reside.

GENERAL ALLEGATIONS

12. In YEAR-2, CFC was preparing to launch a new product called AOA. AOA was an additive to orange juice that was intended to increase the shelf life and improve the taste of orange juice.

13. On October 12, YEAR-2, Alden was attending a meeting with Smart, Henley, and Myers to discuss the results of final product testing of the AOA product. Myers was present via teleconference.

14. At the October 12, YEAR-2meeting, Myers informed the others that the final testing indicated that the AOA product did not work and that the project had to be discontinued.

15. At the same meeting, Alden suggested that the group destroy the test results. Alden also suggested the AOA product launch go ahead despite the negative final test results.

16. At this same meeting, Alden, Smart, Henley, and Myers agreed to continue with the planned AOA product launch despite the negative final test results.

17. During the October 12, YEAR-2meeting, Plaintiff Walter was in the hallway outside the conference room and heard the discussion.

18. On October 26, YEAR-2, Alden held a press conference during which they announced the launch of the AOA product. Alden also stated during the press conference that the final AOA test results were positive despite knowing this was a false statement.

19. CFC, Alden, Smart, Henley, and Myers' decision to destroy the AOA test results and launch the product under the false pretense that the final test results were positive was a violation of a law, rule, or regulation.

20. In March YEAR-1, Plaintiff Walter reported their concerns regarding the content of Alden, Smart, Henley, and Myers' October 12, YEAR-2meeting to Smith, CFC's head of corporate compliance and human resources.

21. Smith conducted an investigation into Plaintiff Walter's allegations and, on April 8, YEAR-1, sent Walter a letter stating that the investigation was concluded and "appropriate action was taken regarding those who acted improperly." Plaintiff Walter was never informed regarding what, if any, action was taken against Alden, Smart, Henley, and Myers as a result of this investigation.

22. On October 1, YEAR-1, Plaintiff Walter was terminated from CFC.

23. Plaintiff Walter's termination was in retaliation for their reporting the AOA matter, which represented a violation of a law, rule, or regulation, to CFC's corporate compliance and human resources department.

COUNT 1
VIOLATION OF THE FLORIDA WHISTLEBLOWER ACT
SECTION 448.101 et seq., FLORIDA STATUTES
(DEFENDANT CFC)

24. Plaintiff Walter re-alleges and incorporates the allegations of paragraphs one (1) through twenty-three (23) above.

25. Section 448.102(3), Florida Statutes, expressly provides a cause of action for any employee who has been the object of a retaliatory personnel action for objecting to or refusing to participate in any activity, policy, or practice of the employer which is in violation of law, rule, or regulation.

26. At all times material to this action, Walter was an employee within the meaning of section 448.101(2), in that they performed services for and under the control and

direction of an employer for wages and other remuneration.

27. At all times material to this action, CFC was an "employer" within the meaning of section 448.101(3) in that CFC is a Corporation that regulatory employed ten (10) or more persons.

28. Defendant CFC retaliated against Plaintiff Walter by terminating their employment after they objected to an activity, policy, or practice of Defendants' that was in violation of a law, rule, or regulation.

29. Plaintiff Walter's termination was in violation of the Florida Whistle Blower Act.

30. As a direct and proximate result of Defendant CFC's violation of the Florida Whistle Blower Act, Plaintiff Walter has suffered damages, including, but not limited to, loss of income, lost wages and benefits, and damages to their personal and professional reputation, damage to their standing in the community, emotional distress, embarrassment, humiliation, and other non-pecuniary injuries.

COUNT 2
CIVIL CONSPIRACY
(DEFENDANTS ALDEN, SMART, HENLEY, MYERS, AND SMITH)

31. Plaintiff Walter re-alleges and incorporates the allegations of paragraphs one (1) through twenty-three (23) above.

32. Where a defendant has entered an agreement with one or more persons to perform an unlawful act or a lawful act by unlawful means and where an overt act in furtherance of the conspiracy is performed and the conspiracy results in damage to the plaintiff, the defendant is liable for civil conspiracy.

33. Defendants Alden, Smart, Henley, Myers, and Smith entered into an agreement to unlawfully retaliate against Plaintiff Walter for objecting to or refusing to participate in an

activity, policy, or practice of CFC's which was in violation of law, rule, or regulation.

34. Defendants Alden, Smart, Henley, Myers, and Smith committed numerous overt acts in furtherance of the conspiracy, including terminating Plaintiff Walter's employment on October 1, YEAR-1.

35. As a direct and proximate result of Defendant Alden, Smart, Henley, Myers, and Smith's civil conspiracy, Plaintiff Walter has suffered damages, including, but not limited to, loss of income, lost wages and benefits, and damages to their personal and professional reputation, damage to their standing in the community, emotional distress, embarrassment, humiliation, and other non-pecuniary injuries.

DEMAND FOR RELIEF

WHEREFORE, Plaintiff, LOGAN WALTER, respectfully demands judgment against Defendants CFC, Alden, Smart, Henley, Myers, and Smith for lost wages and benefits, prejudgment interests, attorney's fees and costs of this action, and all other compensatory damages allowed under law. Plaintiff, LOGAN WALTER, also respectfully demands reinstatement and back pay. Plaintiff, LOGAN WALTER, also respectfully demands such other relief as the Court deems just and proper.

DEMAND FOR JURY TRIAL

Plaintiff, LOGAN WALTER, respectfully demands a trial by jury on all issues so triable.

Dated this 15th day of October, YEAR-1.

Respectfully Submitted

s/ Jan Smartz
Jan Smartz, Esq.
Florida Bar No. 12345
Smartz and Associates, P.A.
123 Apple Way
Tampa, Florida 33601

Attachment B

THE TAMPA GAZETTE & NEWS

"PRINTING THE GOOD, THE BAD, & THE UGLY"

OCTOBER 20,

YEAR-1

Suit Claims that CFC Juiced Folks

By Ali Angelo, Gazette Staff Writer

TAMPA - Citrus Florida Community Company former employee Wayne Logan filed what could be a multi-million dollar lawsuit this week claiming that they were wrongfully fired in retaliation for reporting that several individuals at CFC scammed the public.

The suit claims that CFC raised orange juice prices this past year claiming that a product used in making the orange juice would keep it fresher than other juices on the market. Logan alleges that such a product never existed.

For two months this year, CFC advertised that its juice had a longer shelf life. Many of the juice containers sold during this period claimed that CFC's juice lasted longer than other juices on the market. Company officials said this justified charging more for each container of juice.

Logan, a member of CFC's marketing team, reported to the Tampa company headquarters that several individuals in marketing were well aware that the juice did not have any special ability to last longer.

Logan said that when company officials found out that the new additive being used in the orange juice did not work, they decided to sell the product without telling anyone of the problem.

Logan said that they reported what they knew to the company and officials investigated. Several months later, they said, they were fired.

In addition to suing the company, Logan named specific individuals at CFC who they say were in on the alleged scam. They claimed that Ashley Alden, head of product development at CFC, told Dr. Sami Myers, a scientific researcher for CFC, to destroy the test results so that others would not find out about the inability of the additive to prolong the juice's life.

Logan also named their boss, Chris Smart, the head of the marketing team, and Jess Henley, the head of the sales team, as being involved in this scam.

Logan claims that they had been seriously hurt by being fired from their job at CFC and has been unable to find other employment. They said their house is in foreclosure proceedings.

CFC refused to comment when asked about the lawsuit other than to say that they would not comment on personnel matters.

Attachment C

IN THE UNITED STATES DISTRICT COURT
MIDDLE DISTRICT OF FLORIDA
TAMPA DIVISION

IN THE MATTER OF THE SEARCH OF	)	
1941 LAY ROAD, TAMPA, FL 33601; and	)	CASE NO.
2005 MADOFF STREET, GULFPORT, FL 33707	)	

AFFIDAVIT IN SUPPORT OF WARRANT APPLICATION

I, Bernie Bentham, the undersigned affiant, being first duly sworn, depose and say:

I. INTRODUCTION

1. I am a Special Agent with the Federal Bureau of Investigation (hereafter "FBI") and have been so employed for approximately fourteen years. I am currently assigned to the Tampa, Florida resident agency of the FBI's Central Florida division. In my capacity as an FBI agent, I am authorized to investigate violations of federal law, including, but not limited to Mail Fraud (18 U.S.C. § 1341), Wire Fraud (18 U.S.C. § 1343), Honest Services Fraud (18 U.S.C. § 1346), Securities Fraud (18 U.S.C. § 1348), Insider Trading (15 U.S.C. §§ 78a *et seq.*), Obstruction of Justice (18 U.S.C. §§ 1503, 1505, 1512, and 1519), False Statements (18 U.S.C. § 1001).

2. During my tenure as an FBI agent, I have participated in excess of one hundred federal criminal investigations and prosecutions involving individuals and/or organizations. The statements and information contained in this affidavit are based upon my personal knowledge, information provided by Citrus Florida Community Company employee Logan Walter, information provided by other law enforcement officers and federal agents, and civilians throughout the course of this investigation, and on my experience, knowledge, training, and background as an FBI Agent.

3. Throughout this investigation, affiant has worked with and relied upon numerous other federal agents and agencies collaborating with this investigation. Any reference in this affidavit to information collected by any agent other than the affiant is based upon reports and briefings prepared by the law enforcement agent receiving the information, and the agent's reports and briefings were communicated directly to the affiant.

4. Affiant is presently assisting in an investigation involving a scheme to defraud consumers and retailers of their money and property. Perpetrating this scheme is the Citrus Florida Community Company ("CFC") and its employees, including Ashley Alden ("Alden"), head of CFC's product distribution division, Chris Smart ("Smart"), head of the CFC's marketing team, Jess Henley ("Henley"), head of CFC's sales team, and Dr. Sami Myers, head of CFC's research facility in

Gulfport, Florida.

5. Affiant respectfully submits this affidavit in support of a search warrant application for two (2) warrants to search the two (2) premises described as:

    1) CITRUS FLORIDA COMMUNITY COMPANY
    HEADQUARTERS
    1941 LAY ROAD TAMPA,
    FL 33601; and

    2) CITRUS FLORIDA COMMUNITY COMPANYRESEARCH
    FACILITY
    2005 MADOFF STREET,
    GULFPORT, FL 33707

    for evidence, fruits, and instrumentalities of violations of: a) Title 18, United States Code, Section 1341, (mail fraud); b) Title 18, United States Code, Section 1343, (wire fraud); c) Title 18, United States Code, Section 1346, (honest services fraud); d) Title 18, United States Code, Section 1348 (securities fraud); e) Title 18, United States Code, Section 1503, (obstruction of justice); and f) Title 18, United States Code, Section 371, (conspiracy).

II. BACKGROUND

6. CFC is a major international company that produces, distributes, and ships goods substantially impacting interstate commerce. In addition to other products, CFC produces and distributes in interstate commerce a brand of orange juice, orange cleaning supplies, and orange based air fresheners. CFC operates processing plants throughout the Southeast United States and has approximately eight- thousand employees. CFC products are shipped worldwide and CFC operates an office in New York. In Georgia, CFC operates a packaging plant that employees approximately six-hundred people. In addition, approximately one-hundred and fifty people are employed by CFC at the Tampa, FL headquarters. CFC also operates a research and development facility in Gulfport, FL. The research and development facility is directed by Dr. Sami Myers, the supervisor of the approximately fifty CFC employees at the facility.

7. Prior to October 26, YEAR-2, CFC began experimenting with an orange juice additive known as AOA. AOA was designed to extend the shelf life of CFC's orange juice product thereby increasing the time the product would remain fresh before spoiling. This would consequently increase the amount of time that retailers would keep CFC orange juice for sale to the public, and thus increase the profits of CFC. The company intended to market and financially benefit from this new additive by affixing "AOA" labels to orange juice containers while simultaneously increasing the price for the product. With the promise of a fresher, longer lasting orange juice, an aggressive marketing campaign, and the new AOA label attached, CFC sold orange juice for an additional one dollar per liter.

CFC discontinued production of AOA approximately two months after the product was introduced to the public.

III. INVESTIGATION AND PROBABLY CAUSE

8. The facts establishing probable cause for the issuance of this search warrant are as follows. On or about October 20, YEAR-1, newspaper columnist Ali Angelo authored an article in *The Tampa Gazette & News* detailing widespread fraud and unlawful conduct on the part of CFC employees. According to the article, Logan Walter, a former CFC employee, filed a civil suit against CFC challenging their termination from CFC. Walter received their termination letter on or about October 1, YEAR-1, and believes that they were fired for reporting to company officials the unlawful and fraudulent conduct of several CFC employees.

9. Affiant has substantial reason to believe that on or about October 12, YEAR-2, multiple employees of CFC assembled in the company conference room at the corporate headquarters of CFC in Tampa, FL. CFC employees Alden, Smart, and Henley were all present at the October 12, YEAR-2 meeting. Alden, with Smart and Henley in the room, then spoke with Dr. Myers on the telephone. The conversation concerned the additive known as "AOA." During this telephone conversation on or about October 12, YEAR-2, Alden was told by Dr. Myers that the final test results showed that the AOA additive was useless and ineffective and therefore the AOA additive project must be cancelled. Affiant has substantial reason to believe that after discussion and in agreement with Smart and Henley, Alden ordered Dr. Myers to destroy the final AOA test results, which were housed at CFC's research facility and which illustrated the defective nature of AOA.

10. Affiant has interviewed Logan Walter, a CFC employee who overheard the above described telephone conversation between Alden, Smart, Henley, and Dr. Myers.

11. On or about October 26, YEAR-2, Alden announced at a press conference that the final test results show that AOA was effective and would soon be sold nationally. At this press conference, affiant has substantial reason to believe that Alden fraudulently misled investors regarding the effectiveness of the AOA additive. Following this announcement, CFC sold orange juice to retailers at an increased price claiming the product contained AOA and AOA was effective.

12. Based on the foregoing facts, and after interviewing Walter, affiant has substantial reason to believe that CFC employees, including, but not limited to, Alden, Smart, Henley, and Dr. Myers, have engaged in violations of federal law, including, but not limited to Mail Fraud (18 U.S.C. § 1341), Wire Fraud (18 U.S.C. § 1343), Honest Services Fraud (18 U.S.C. § 1346), Securities Fraud (18 U.S.C. § 1348), Insider Trading (15 U.S.C. §§ 78a *et seq.*), Obstruction of Justice (18 U.S.C. §§ 1503, 1505, 1512, and 1519), False Statements (18 U.S.C. § 1001).

IV. ITEMS TO BE SEIZED

13. Based on these facts and circumstances, affiant believes probable cause exists that evidence, fruits, and instrumentalities of the aforementioned violations exists at the premises' identified as:

    1) CITRUS FLORIDA COMMUNITY COMPANY HEADQUARTERS
    1941 LAY ROAD TAMPA,
    FL 33601; and

    2) CITRUS FLORIDA COMMUNITY COMPANY RESEARCH FACILITY
    2005 MADOFF STREET,
    GULFPORT, FL 33707

14. The items to be seized are as follows:

    a. All documents evidencing a violation of federal law.

    b. All documents located in the offices or work stations of Ashley Alden, Chris Smart, Logan Walter, Jess Henley, Dr. Sami Meyers.

    c. Documents regarding the AOA additive.

    d. Documents regarding orange juice pricing.

    e. Documents regarding orange juice sales agreements and contracts.

    f. All human resources files for Ashley Alden, Chris Smart, Logan Walter, Jess Henley, and Dr. Sami Meyers.

    g. Documents relating to stock options for all CFC employees in the product distribution division, Dr. Myers, Jody Murray, Kim Vanguard, Tracy Strain, and Cory Campbell.

    h. Documents relating to bank accounts, brokerage accounts, and trusts for all CFC employees in the product distribution division, Dr. Myers, Jody Murray, Kim Vanguard, Tracy Strain, and Cory Campbell.

    i. Documents relating to personnel and payroll records for all CFC employees in the product distribution division, Dr. Myers, Jody Murray, Kim Vanguard, Tracy Strain, and Cory Campbell.

Attachment D

j. Documents relating to CFC accounting records.

k. Rolodexes, address books, and calendars for all CFC employees in the product distribution division, Ashley Alden, Chris Smart, Logan Walter, Jess Henley, Dr. Myers, Jody Murray, Kim Vanguard, Tracy Strain, and Cory Campbell.

l. The computers (laptop or desktop) of Ashley Alden, Chris Smart, Logan Walter, Jess Henley, Dr. Sami Meyers, Jody Murray, Kim Vanguard, Tracy Strain, and Cory Campbell.

m. All mobile phones or other communication devices for Ashley Alden, Chris Smart, Logan Walter, Jess Henley, Dr. Sami Meyers, Jody Murray, Kim Vanguard, Tracy Strain, and Cory Campbell.

CERTIFICATE AND SIGNATURES

I certify that the information contained in this affidavit is true and accurate to the best of knowledge and belief.

WHEREFORE, the undersigned requests the issuance of a search warrant for the above-described property.

FURTHER AFFIANT SAYETH NAUGHT

Bernie Bentham

Bernie Bentham
Federal Bureau of Investigation

Signed and sworn to before me in chambers, this 27 day of October, YEAR-1

S. Marshal

HON. S. Marshal
United States Magistrate Judge

IN THE UNITED STATES DISTRICT COURT
MIDDLE DISTRICT OF FLORIDA
TAMPA DIVISION

IN THE MATTER OF THE SEARCH OF 1941 LAY ROAD, TAMPA, FL 33601; and 2005 MADOFF STREET, GULFPORT, FL 33707	)) Case No. 8:12-cr-00019-CFC-TPA)

SEARCH AND SEIZURE WARRANT

To: Any authorized law enforcement officer

An application by a federal law enforcement officer requests the search of the following property located in the Middle District of Florida.

Citrus Florida Community Company Headquarters
1941 Lay Road, Tampa, Florida 33601

AND

Citrus Florida Community Company Research Facility
2005 Madoff Street, Gulfport, Florida 33707

The person or property to be searched, described above, is believed to conceal evidence of the crimes of Mail Fraud (18 U.S.C. § 1341), Wire Fraud (18 U.S.C. § 1343), Honest Services Fraud (18 U.S.C. § 1346), Securities Fraud (18 U.S.C. § 1348), Insider Trading (15 U.S.C. §§ 78a et seq.), Obstruction of Justice (18 U.S.C. §§ 1503, 1505, 1512, and 1519), False Statements (18 U.S.C. § 1001) and property used in committing these offenses.

I find that the affidavit, or any recorded testimony, establishes probable cause to search and seize the property.

YOU ARE COMMANDED to execute this warrant on or before November 1, YEAR-1

☒ in the daytime 6:00 a.m. to 10:00 p.m. ☐ at any time in the day or night as I find reasonable cause has been established

Unless delayed notice is authorized below, you must give a copy of the warrant and a receipt for the property taken to the person from whom, or from whose premises, the property was taken, or leave the copy and receipt at the place where the property was taken.

The officer executing this warrant, or an officer present during the execution of the warrant, must prepare an inventory as required by law and promptly return this warrant and inventory to the United States Magistrate Judge S. Marshal.

Date and time issued:	October 27, YEAR-1 at 4:47 p.m.	*Magistrate Marshal*
City and state:	Tampa, Florida	*Magistrate Marshal*

Attachment E

Return		
Case No:	*Date and time warrant executed:*	*Copy of warrant and inventory left with:*
Inventory made in the presence of:		
Inventory of the property taken and name of any person(s) seized:		

Certification
I declare under penalty of perjury that this inventory is correct and was returned along with the original warrant to the designated judge.

Date: ______________

____
Executing officer's signature

____
Printed name and title

Attachment E

Citrus Florida
Community Company
Corporate Bylaws

Originally Adopted – January 1,
YEAR-18
Last Modified – January 1,
YEAR-3

Excerpted

Article I

Herein follow the corporate bylaws of the Citrus Florida Community Company. The Citrus Florida Community Company and these bylaws are created under the laws of the state of Florida.

...

Article IX

Section 1. Indemnification. (a) The Corporation shall indemnify, to the fullest extent permitted by law, any person made or threatened to be made a party to any threatened, pending, or completed action, lawsuit, or proceeding, whether civil, criminal, administrative, or investigative, by reason of the fact that such person is or was a director or officer of the Corporation.

(b) The Corporation may indemnify, to the fullest extent permitted by law, any person made or threatened to be made a party to any threatened, pending, or completed action, lawsuit, or proceeding, whether civil, criminal, administrative, or investigative, by reason of the fact that such person is or was an employee or agent of the Corporation.

Section 2. Advancement of Expenses. (a) Regarding any director or officer of the Corporation made or threatened to be made a party to any threatened, pending, or completed proceeding, by reason of the fact that such person is or was a director or officer of the Corporation, the Corporation shall pay expenses (including reasonable attorney's fees) incurred by such person in defending any such proceeding in advance of its final disposition. (Added January 1, YEAR-3).

(b) Regarding any employee of the Corporation made or threatened to be made a party to any threatened, pending, or completed proceeding, by reason of the fact that such person is or was an employee of the Corporation, the Corporation may, in its sole discretion and upon such terms and conditions, if any, as the Corporation deems appropriate, pay expenses (including reasonable attorney's fees) incurred by such person in defending any such proceeding in advance of its final disposition. (Added January 1, YEAR-3).

(c) Any advancement of expenses under Article IX, Section 2 of these bylaws shall be made only upon receipt of a written agreement by such person to repay all amounts advanced if it shall ultimately be determined by final judgment that such person is not entitled to indemnification as provided for in Article IX of these bylaws. (Added January 1, YEAR-3).

Attachment F

Section 3. Determination of Entitlement to Indemnification. Indemnification under Article IX shall be made only upon a determination that indemnification is proper because the director, officer or employee has met all applicable standards of conduct required by law.

CODE OF FLORIDA

TITLE 10. CORPORATIONS CHAPTER
1. GENERAL CORPORATION LAW
SUBCHAPTER X. DIRECTORS AND OFFICERS

10 Florida § 101*
(YEAR-1)

§ 101. Indemnification of officers, directors, employees and agents

(1) A corporation shall have power to indemnify any person who was or is a party to any proceeding (other than an action by, or in the right of, the corporation), by reason of the fact that he or she is or was a director, officer, employee, or agent of the corporation or is or was serving at the request of the corporation as a director, officer, employee, or agent of another corporation, partnership, joint venture, trust, or other enterprise against liability incurred in connection with such proceeding, including any appeal thereof, if he or she acted in good faith and in a manner he or she reasonably believed to be in, or not opposed to, the best interests of the corporation and, with respect to any criminal action or proceeding, had no reasonable cause to believe his or her conduct was unlawful. The termination of any proceeding by judgment, order, settlement, or conviction or upon a plea of nolo contendere or its equivalent shall not, of itself, create a presumption that the person did not act in good faith and in a manner which he or she reasonably believed to be in, or not opposed to, the best interests of the corporation or, with respect to any criminal action or proceeding, had reasonable cause to believe that his or her conduct was unlawful.

(2) A corporation shall have power to indemnify any person, who was or is a party to any proceeding by or in the right of the corporation to procure a judgment in its favor by reason of the fact that the person is or was a director, officer, employee, or agent of the corporation or is or was serving at the request of the corporation as a director, officer, employee, or agent of another corporation, partnership, joint venture, trust, or other enterprise, against expenses and amounts paid in settlement not exceeding, in the judgment of the board of directors, the estimated expense of litigating the proceeding to conclusion, actually and reasonably incurred in connection with the defense or settlement of such proceeding, including any appeal thereof. Such indemnification shall be authorized if such person acted in good faith and in a manner he or she reasonably believed to be in, or not opposed to, the best interests of the corporation, except that no indemnification shall be made under this subsection in respect of any claim, issue, or matter as to which such person shall have been adjudged to be liable unless, and only to the extent that, the court in which such proceeding was brought, or any other court of competent jurisdiction, shall determine upon application that, despite the adjudication of liability but in view of all circumstances of the case, such person is fairly and reasonably entitled to indemnity for such expenses which such court shall deem proper.

(3) To the extent that a director, officer, employee, or agent of a corporation has been successful on the merits or otherwise in defense of any proceeding referred to in subsection (1) or subsection (2), or in defense of any claim, issue, or matter therein, he or she shall be indemnified against expenses actually and reasonably incurred by him or her in connection therewith.

(4) Any indemnification under subsection (1) or subsection (2), unless pursuant to a determination by a court, shall be made by the corporation only as authorized in the specific case upon a determination that indemnification of the director, officer, employee, or agent is proper in the circumstances because he or she has met the applicable standard of conduct set forth in subsection (1) or subsection (2). Such determination shall be made:

(a) By the board of directors by a majority vote of a quorum consisting of directors who were not parties to such proceeding;

(b) If such a quorum is not obtainable or, even if obtainable, by majority vote of a committee duly designated by the board of directors (in which directors who are parties may participate) consisting solely of two or more directors not at the time parties to the proceeding;

(c) By independent legal counsel:

1. Selected by the board of directors prescribed in paragraph (a) or the committee prescribed in paragraph (b); or

2. If a quorum of the directors cannot be obtained for paragraph (a) and the committee cannot be designated under paragraph (b), selected by majority vote of the full board of directors (in which directors who are parties may participate); or

(d) By the shareholders by a majority vote of a quorum consisting of shareholders who were not parties to such proceeding or, if no such quorum is obtainable, by a majority vote of shareholders who were not parties to such proceeding.

(5) Evaluation of the reasonableness of expenses and authorization of indemnification shall be made in the same manner as the determination that indemnification is permissible. However, if the determination of permissibility is made by independent legal counsel, persons specified by paragraph (4)(c) shall evaluate the reasonableness of expenses and may authorize indemnification.

(6) Expenses incurred by an officer or director in defending a civil or criminal proceeding may be paid by the corporation in advance of the final disposition of such proceeding upon receipt of an undertaking by or on behalf of such director or officer to repay such amount if he or she is ultimately found not to be entitled to indemnification by the corporation pursuant to this section. Expenses incurred by other employees and agents may be paid in advance upon such terms or conditions that the board of directors deems appropriate.

(7) The indemnification and advancement of expenses provided pursuant to this section are not exclusive, and a corporation may make any other or further indemnification or advancement of expenses of any of its directors, officers, employees, or agents, under any bylaw, agreement, vote of shareholders or disinterested directors, or otherwise, both as to action in his or her official capacity and as to action in another capacity while holding such office. However, indemnification or advancement of expenses shall not be made to or on behalf of any director, officer, employee, or agent if a judgment or other final adjudication establishes that his or her actions, or omissions to act, were material to the cause of action so adjudicated and constitute:

(a) A violation of the criminal law, unless the director, officer, employee, or agent had reasonable cause to believe his or her conduct was lawful or had no reasonable cause to believe his or her conduct was unlawful;

(b) A transaction from which the director, officer, employee, or agent derived an improper personal benefit;

(c) In the case of a director, a circumstance under which the liability provisions of s. 607.0834 are applicable; or

(d) Willful misconduct or a conscious disregard for the best interests of the corporation in a proceeding by or in the right of the corporation to procure a judgment in its favor or in a proceeding by or in the right of a shareholder.

(8) Indemnification and advancement of expenses as provided in this section shall continue as, unless otherwise provided when authorized or ratified, to a person who has ceased to be a director, officer, employee, or agent and shall inure to the benefit of the heirs, executors, and administrators of such a person, unless otherwise provided

when authorized or ratified.

(9) Unless the corporation's articles of incorporation provide otherwise, notwithstanding the failure of a corporation to provide indemnification, and despite any contrary determination of the board or of the shareholders in the specific case, a director, officer, employee, or agent of the corporation who is or was a party to a proceeding may apply for indemnification or advancement of expenses, or both, to the court conducting the proceeding, to the circuit court, or to another court of competent jurisdiction. On receipt of an application, the court, after giving any notice that it considers necessary, may order indemnification and advancement of expenses, including expenses incurred in seeking court-ordered indemnification or advancement of expenses, if it determines that:

(a) The director, officer, employee, or agent is entitled to mandatory indemnification under subsection (3), in which case the court shall also order the corporation to pay the director reasonable expenses incurred in obtaining court-ordered indemnification or advancement of expenses;

(b) The director, officer, employee, or agent is entitled to indemnification or advancement of expenses, or both, by virtue of the exercise by the corporation of its power pursuant to subsection (7); or

(c) The director, officer, employee, or agent is fairly and reasonably entitled to indemnification or advancement of expenses, or both, in view of all the relevant circumstances, regardless of whether such person met the standard of conduct set forth in subsection (1), subsection (2), or subsection (7).

(10) For purposes of this section, the term "corporation" includes, in addition to the resulting corporation, any constituent corporation (including any constituent of a constituent) absorbed in a consolidation or merger, so that any person who is or was a director, officer, employee, or agent of a constituent corporation, or is or was serving at the request of a constituent corporation as a director, officer, employee, or agent of another corporation, partnership, joint venture, trust, or other enterprise, is in the same position under this section with respect to the resulting or surviving corporation as he or she would have with respect to such constituent corporation if its separate existence had continued.

[Note: This statute is provided for this trial problem only and is not intended to accurately represent any Florida laws]

Employment Agreement
Between the Citrus Florida Community Company (CFC) and Dr. Sami Myers

By and between the Citrus Florida Community Company (hereinafter "CFC" or "Company") and Dr. Sami Myers (hereinafter "Employee").

The Company, located in Tampa, Florida, employs Employee and Employee hereby agrees to the following terms and conditions of employment:

1. Employment shall commence on October 1, YEAR-7.
2. Employee shall serve as head of the CFC Research Facility, located in Gulfport, Florida. Employee's duties shall include, but not be limited to, the following:
    a. Supervise employees of the CFC Research Facility;
    b. Conduct, supervise, and oversee research as directed by CFC;
    c. Ensure the CFC Research Facility remains in compliance with generally accepted scientific standards for the research being conducted;
    d. Present research findings, conclusions, and recommendations to CFC management; and
    e. Employee shall also perform such other duties as are customary and necessary for the position of appointment.
3. To the extent permitted by law and consistent with CFC's bylaws, Employee shall be indemnified and advanced expenses if employee is made or threatened to be made a party to any civil, criminal, administrative, or investigative action, suit, or proceeding by reason of the fact that such person is or was an employee of the Company.
4. This employment agreement shall remain in effect until it is terminated by either party at their sole discretion.
5. Employee agrees not to disclose any of the Company's trade secrets or other confidential information to third parties. Any violation of this provision shall result in the immediate termination of the employee pursuant to article 4 of this agreement.
6. This employment agreement is created and executed pursuant to the laws of the state of Florida.

In witness whereof, both parties have executed this agreement at CFC's Tampa Headquarters on September 19, YEAR-7.

ABA on behalf of CFC

Citrus Florida Community Company

Dr. Sami Myers

Dr. Sami Myers

Attachment G

Citrus Florida Community Company
Since 1895

Jody Murray
Chief Executive Officer
Citrus Florida
Community Company
Tampa, Florida

November 3, YEAR-1

To: All CFC Employees in the Product Distribution Division; All CFC Employees in the Human Resources Division; and All Corporate Officers and Directors

Re: **IMPORTANT** information regarding document retention

Dear CFC employee,

As you may know, the government recently conducted a search of the CFC Tampa headquarters and Gulfport research facility. To ensure materials relevant to the subject of this government inquiry are preserved, please suspend all document destruction protocols immediately and carefully review this memorandum for further instructions.

We must ensure that all documents relevant to this matter are maintained, and we appreciate your cooperation in this effort. If you do not understand something or have any question about anything please contact the General Counsel's office at 321-555-0000.

Document Retention Policy

Generally, CFC's document retention policy sets forth guidelines for how long we keep each type of document. For example, all accounting records are maintained for seven years and, after that period, they are destroyed. To read the entirety of the document retention policy, please refer to Chapter Seven, Subsection B of your Employee Handbook.

The document retention policy also sets forth specific requirements for implementation when the company is facing pending or threatened litigation or a government investigation. These

Attachment H

provisions are found under Section Eight of the policy, which is reproduced below.

Section 8 – Suspension Because of Pending Investigation/Litigation

> **(a)** In the event of any pending or threatened litigation or government investigation, the CFO of CFC will send all employees a memorandum ordering the suspension of all related document destruction. This memorandum should contain a detailed description of documents and other items to be saved. All efforts should be made to preserve any documents or other items that are pertinent and related to the investigation/litigation.
>
> **(b)** In the event the scope of the government investigation is uncertain, the company shall cease destruction of ALL documents in the impacted units/divisions until the scope of the matter is defined or the matter is concluded.
>
> **(d)** Routine document destruction protocols <u>shall not</u> be resumed without written instruction from the Chief Executive Officer or the General Counsel's Office.

CFC has currently reached a point at which section 8(b) is applicable. Because the extent of the government investigation is, as of yet, unknown, please immediately cease all document destruction protocols and preserve all documents until notified otherwise according to the procedures described herein.

<u>What Documents or Materials Must be Preserved?</u>

This document preservation memorandum applies to all company documents or materials within your possession or control, both hard copy and electronic.

The term documents and materials covers a wide variety of things. These include electronic documents, emails, paper documents, notes, sticky notes, voicemails, audio recordings, and so on. Below is a non-exhaustive list of things that must be preserved if they fall within any of the related categories:

published materials	reports
correspondence	emails
records	memoranda
notices	notes
marginal notations	message
teletype printouts	statements
books	studies

minutes	diagrams
drawing	maps
surveys	plans
charts	graphs
data	computer files
computer tapes	computer discs
computer printouts	computer hard drives
appointment books	telephone messages and message tapes
telephone message slips	drafts
checks	money orders
invoices	billings
evaluations	photographs
audio tapes	videotapes
electronically stored information	

If you have any doubts or are unsure whether something should be persevered, DO NOT destroy or dispose of it. Ask your supervisor and wait until you receive an answer before taking any action.

Specific Actions That Must Be Taken

Aside from suspending all existing document destruction protocols, there are several affirmative actions that must be taken.

Automatic Deletions of Emails and Electronic Documents

First, the information technology department must change settings on emails and electronic documents so that they do not automatically delete after a certain period of time. If you notice any emails or documents being deleted from your computers, please contact your supervisor immediately. Additionally, if you have specific settings on your computer to delete anything, please remove it or alert the IT department immediately so they can suspend the setting to ensure nothing is deleted.

Destruction of Originals When Converting Into Electronic Documents

It is CFC policy to destroy some original documents when converting them into electronic format. Although the practice of converting documents should continue, make sure that you do not destroy or alter any originals. Please contact your supervisor for specific procedures and policies that your particular department will be implementing.

Preservation of Documents and Items Taken Home By Employees

According to company policy, many employees are permitted to take home specific work assignments, company equipment, or have work-related items stored on your home computer. Be sure to take any and all steps to ensure that these things are preserved. You may or may not be asked to bring one or all of these things in and have them reviewed.

Questions

If you have any questions regarding the government investigation, anything relating to the preservation or destruction of documents, please contact the General Counsel's office at 321-555-0000.

I would like to thank you for your cooperation and your patience.

Sincerely,

s/ Jody Murray

Jody Murray
Chief Executive Officer

Attachment H

Acknowledgement of Receipt of Document Retention Memorandum and Understanding of Responsibilities

I, ________________________, have read and understand the document retention memorandum sent to Citrus Florida Community Company employees on November 3, YEAR-1. I further understand the failure to comply with this memo and the document retention policy may result in my termination or suspension.

I understand that it is the policy of CFC that all existing document destruction protocols should be immediately suspended and all documents must heretofore be preserved until I am otherwise notified byJody Murray or the CFC General Counsel's Office.

Date: ____

Employee Name, Printed: ________________________________

Employee Signature: __________________________________

Signature of Supervisor: _________________________________

Received By Litigation Response Team: ____________________

Attachment H

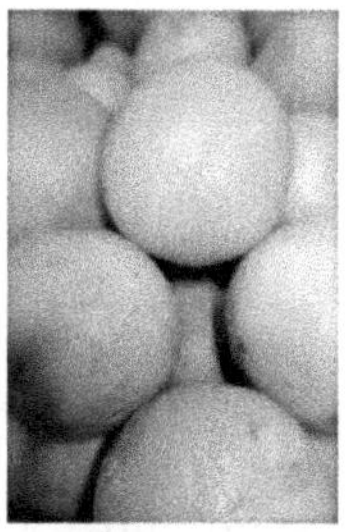

Citrus Florida Community Company
Since 1895

Cory Campbell
General Counsel
Citrus Florida Community Company
Tampa, Florida

November 3, YEAR-1

To: All CFC Employees

Re: **IMPORTANT** Information Regarding Document Search Memorandum

---

Dear CFC employee,

As you may know, the government recently conducted a search of the CFC Tampa headquarters and Gulfport research facility. To assist CFC's outside counsel in conducting a review of documents and materials related to this government inquiry, the company requests your assistance in collecting documents and materials related to the subject of the government investigation. Once collected, these materials must be sent to the CFC General Counsel's Office for review.

Please review this memorandum carefully and comply with its requests within **five business days**. You will find a certification document on the last page of this memorandum. Please review and sign this certification and return it with your collected documents and materials. If you do not understand something or have any question about anything, please contact the General Counsel's office at 321-555-0000.

Documents for Collection

The government's investigation currently focusses on the sale of orange juice and the use of the AOA additive. Therefore, please collect and provide to the General Counsel's Office any documents or materials related to the following:

(1) All documents and materials regarding the additive AOA. This includes, but is not limited to, the following:

Attachment I

a. All documents and materials regarding scientific research (raw data, reports, memoranda, presentations etc.)
b. All documents and materials regarding marketing
c. All documents and materials relating to or reflecting agreements or contracts for the sale or purchase of products containing AOA
d. All documents and materials regarding the pricing of products containing AOA
e. All documents and materials containing financial data regarding products containing AOA (sales data, reports, memoranda, presentations etc.)

(2) All materials and documents regarding scientific research conducted on CFC orange juice since YEAR-12.
(3) All documents and materials regarding marketing of CFC orange juice since YEAR-12.
(4) All documents and materials relating to or reflecting agreements or contracts for the sale or purchase of CFC orange juice since YEAR-12.
(5) All documents and materials regarding the pricing of CFC orange juice since YEAR-12.
(6) All documents and materials containing financial data regarding CFC orange juice.
(7) All documents and materials regarding official communications between CFC employees and market analysts, stock holders, and/or stock brokers.
(8) All documents and materials regarding CFC's reduction in force in October YEAR-1.

Where documents or materials are maintained in hard copy format, please provide the originals. Where originals are contained within a file, please provide the entire file with the original document or material remaining within the file. Should you require use of any hard copy documents or materials provided, please make copies of such documents or materials prior to providing them to the General Counsel's Office.

Where documents or materials are maintained in electronic format, including email, please provide printed copies of the documents or materials. Then ensure that the original electronic version of the document or material is preserved until informed otherwise. Where a large volume of relevant electronic materials makes printing impractical, please provide a copy of the documents on a portable hard drive or upload the documents through the link provided via email today entitled "Cloud Data Upload Link Email."

Questions

If you have any questions regarding the government investigation, anything relating to the preservation or destruction of documents, or this document search memorandum please contact the General Counsel's office at 321-555-0000.

I would like to thank you for your cooperation and your patience.

Sincerely,

s/ Cory Campbell

Cory Campbell
General Counsel

Tomi Bell Interview Notes – Interview of Jamie Tate (November 9, YEAR-1)

- Gave Corporate Miranda.
- Tate on Sales Team:
  - Headed by Jess Henley.
  - 20 people on team.
  - Henley reports to Alden.
- Involved in AOA product roll out in late YEAR-2. AOA suppose to (a) prolong shelf life and (b) make juice last longer (equals better tasting). Alden constantly talked about the product – "obsessed."
- Launch press conference:
  - Late October YEAR-2.
  - Tate and others present from Production Division.
  - Press present for announcement.
  - Banner, boxes of OJ with stamp etc.
  - Alden said test results were good. "Wild success." Retail customers "snapping" up the new product.
- After the launch:
  - Big push to sell. Especially in first month.
  - Two months later product pulled. Profit issue.
  - "One day we were pushing this product everywhere and the next day it was gone."
- Henley?
  - Alden's inner circle.
    - Henley, Smart, Alden
    - Always meeting. Probably discussing AOA. Not sure.
  - Attitude? Signs of distraction/uncomfortable?
    - "Upset" about something around time of AOA launch.
    - Fight in hallway with Smart. "You do what you want, but this whole testing mess doesn't sit right with me." Unsure what talking about.
  - During product launch Henley in back of room. "Very uneasy."
- Anyone else asked about issue?
  - No one specifically.
  - Henley once said in passing when they were discussing an unrelated issue in Henley's office, "If anyone from compliance ever comes down here, make sure you tell the truth. Don't lie for me, I haven't done anything wrong and I'm not sticking my neck out for anyone either." Tate found it strange, but didn't inquire further and doesn't know what Henley meant. Thinks it may have related to some harassment investigation of Alden a year earlier.
  - Heard rumor Lynn Smith did investigation of AOA. Not sure. Didn't talk to Tate.
- Anything else? No.

Attachment J

Interview Memorandum

To: CFC File – Matter Number YEAR-1.0035

From: Tomi Bell, White Collar Team, Bell & Bell LLP

Re: Interview Memorandum of Jamie Tate (Member, Sales Team, Citrus Florida Community Company)

Date: November 10, YEAR-1

On November 9, YEAR-1 Tomi Bell (Attorney, White Collar Team, Bell & Bell LLP) interviewed Jamie Tate (Member, Sales Team, Citrus Florida Community Company) at the Citrus Florida Community Company offices in Tampa, Florida. This memorandum is created in anticipation of litigation and contains the attorney's mental impressions and conclusions.

The Citrus Florida Community Company ("CFC") was founded in 1895 as a small citrus processing entity. Over the decades, however, the company expanded into all areas of the citrus industry, including the production of their own orange juice brands, orange cleaning supply products, orange based air fresheners and other products with a citrus base. Currently, CFC distributes its materials to numerous national store chains and employs eight-thousand people. Approximately one-hundred and fifty people work at CFC's headquarters in Tampa, Florida.

Jamie Tate is a member of the CFC Sales Team, located in the Tampa, Florida headquarters. The Sales Team is headed by Jess Henley (Head, Sales Team, CFC). The sales team consists of twenty employees under the leadership of Henley.

Tate recalls that in late YEAR-2 CFC was excited about the prospects of launching a new orange juice additive called AOA. According to Tate, the additive was designed to prolong the shelf life of orange juice and, simultaneously, lengthen the time before the orange juice spoils. According to Tate, this all meant the juice would taste fresher longer.

Tate recalls that in October YEAR-2, Ashley Alden (Head, Product Distribution Division) would constantly talk about the AOA additive in Product Distribution Division meetings. In Tate's opinion, it appeared that Alden was "obsessed" with the product. Sometime in late October YEAR-2, Tate and every other member of the Production Division attended a large launch press conference for the AOA product. Tate recalls a huge banner, boxes of orange juice with the new AOA symbol, and press everywhere. At the press conference, Tate believes Alden told the crowd that test results showed that the new product was a "wild success" and that retail customers were already "snapping" the new product up.

According to Tate, there was a big push to sell as much of the orange juice as possible in the first month. Finally, after about two months, the product was discontinued because it wasn't showing a sufficient profit. Tate noted, "One day we were pushing this product everywhere and the next day it was gone."

When asked about the role of Tate's supervisor, Henley, in the launch of the AOA additive, Tate noted that Henley was part of Alden's "inner circle." Henley, Chris Smart (Head, Marketing Team), and Alden were always meeting. Tate does not have first-hand knowledge of what was discussed at these meetings, but believes they were likely discussing AOA much of the time during the launch period.

When asked about Henley's attitude and demeanor around the time of the AOA launch, Tate noted that Henley appeared "upset" about something. Specifically, Tate recalls hearing Henley and Smart having a loud argument in the hallway. Tate is unsure what they were discussing, but Tate recalls Henley stating, "This whole testing mess doesn't sit right with me." Tate does not know what testing was being referred to by Henley. Tate also recalls that Henley was standing in the back of the room during the AOA launch press conference and looked "very uneasy."

Tate was asked whether anyone had previously interviewed or asked questions about the AOA additive. Tate stated that no one had asked them anything specific about the product. However, Tate had heard rumors that Lynn Smith (Head, Corporate Compliance) was interviewing people about the additive in early YEAR-1.

Tate was asked if there was anything else we should know about this matter or any other matters at the company. Tate responded that there was nothing else.

United States District Court

MIDDLE	DISTRICT OF	FLORIDA

TO: Citrus Florida
Community Company
1941 Lay Road
Tampa, Florida 33601

SUBPOENA TO TESTIFY
BEFORE GRAND JURY

SUBPOENA FOR:

☐ PERSON ☒ DOCUMENTS OR OBJECT(S)

YOU ARE HEREBY COMMANDED to appear before the Grand Jury of the United States District Court at the place, date, and time specified below.

PLACE	ROOM
Sam M. Gibbons U.S. Courthouse 801 North Florida Ave. Tampa, Florida 33602	Grand Jury Room DATE AND TIME December 15, YEAR-1

YOU ARE ALSO COMMANDED to bring with you the following document(s) or object(s):*

<u>See</u> Attachment A.

☒ *Please see additional information on following page(s)*

This subpoena shall remain in effect until you are granted to leave to depart by the court or by an officer acting on behalf of the court.

CLERK	DATE
Sheryl L. Loesch, Clerk	
(BY) DEPUTY CLERK Thomas Gates	

This subpoena is issued upon application of the United States of America	* If not applicable, enter "none"

Attachment L

NAME, ADDRESS AND PHONE NUMBER OF ASSISTANT US ATTORNEY

Jo Jones, Assistant United States Attorney

400 North Tampa St., Suite 3200
Tampa, Fl. 33602

RETURN OF SERVICE (1)		
RECEIVED BY SERVER	DATE	PLACE
SERVED	DATE	PLACE

Attachment L

SERVED ON (PRINT NAME)	
SERVED BY (PRINT NAME)	TITLE

STATEMENT OF SERVICE FEES

TRAVEL	SERVICES	TOTAL

DECLARATION OF SERVER [2]

I declare under penalty of perjury under the laws of the United States of Am erica that the foregoing information contained in the Proof of Service is true and correct.

Executed on ______________________ ______________________

DATE SIGNATURE OF SERVER

____

ADDRESS OF SERVER

____

ADDITIONAL INFORMATION

Copies of the requested materials may be delivered to the USAO by the date requested in lieu of appearan ce before the grand jury.

(1) As to who may serve a subpoena and the manner of its service see Rule 17(d), Federal Rules of Criminal Procedure, or Rule 45(c), Federal Rules of Civil Procedure

(2) "Fees and mileage need not be tendered to the witness upon service of a subpoena issues on behalf of the United States or an officer or agency thereof (Rule 45(c), Federal Rules of Civil Procedure) or on behalf of certain indigent parties and criminal defendants who are unable to pay such costs (28 USC 1825, Rule 17(b) Federal Rules of Criminal Procedure)".

Attachment L

DEFINITIONS AND INSTRUCTIONS

A. "You" or "Your" as used herein means any of the respondents, their agents and employees or any "affiliate" of the aforementioned entities, as that term is herein defined.

Your agents include but are not limited to your officers, directors, attorneys, accountants, CPA's, advertising consultants, or advertising account representatives.

Any document in the possession of you, your affiliates, your agents or your employees is deemed to be within your possession or control. You have the affirmative duty to contact your agents, affiliates and employees and to obtain documentation from them, if such documentation is responsive to this subpoena.

B. Unless otherwise indicated, documents to be produced pursuant to this subpoena should include all original documents prepared, sent, dated, received, in effect, or which otherwise came into existence at any time. If your "original" is a photocopy, then the photocopy would be and should be produced as the original.

C. This subpoena duces tecum calls for the production of all responsive documents in your possession, custody or control without regard to the physical location of said documents.

D. "And" and "or" are used as terms of inclusion, not exclusion.

E. The documents to be produced pursuant to each request should be segregated and specifically identified to indicate clearly the particular numbered request to which they are responsive.

F. In the event that you seek to withhold any document on the basis that is properly entitled to some privilege or limitation, please provide the following information:

1. A list identifying each document for which you believe a limitation exists;
2. The name of each author, writer, sender or initiator of such document or thing, if any;
3. The name of each recipient, addressee or party for whom such document or thing was intended, if any;
4. The date of such document, if any, or an estimate thereof so indicated if no date appears on the document;
5. The general subject matter as described in such document, or, if no such description appears, then such other description sufficient to identify said document; and
6. The claimed grounds for withholding the document, including, but not limited to, the nature of any claimed privilege and grounds in support thereof.

G. For each request, or part thereof, which is not fully responded to pursuant to a privilege, the nature of the privilege and grounds in support thereof should be fully stated.

H. If you possess, control or have custody of no documents responsive to any of the numbered requests set forth below, state this fact in your response to said request.

I. For purposes of responding to this subpoena, the term "document" shall mean all writings or stored data or information of any kind, in any form, including the originals and all non-identical copies, whether different from the originals by reason of any notation(s) made on such copies or otherwise, including, without limitation: correspondence, notes, letters, telegrams, minutes, certificates, diplomas, contracts, franchise agreements and other agreements, brochures, pamphlets, forms, scripts, reports, studies, statistics, inter-office and intra-office communications, training materials, analyses, memoranda, statements, summaries, graphs, charts, tests, plans, arrangements, tabulations, bulletins, newsletters, advertisements, computer printouts, teletype, telefax, microfilm, e-mail, electronically stored data, price books and lists, invoices, receipts, inventories, regularly kept summaries or compilations of business records, notations of any type of conversations, meetings, telephone or other communications, audio and videotapes; electronic, mechanical or electrical records or representations of any kind (including without limitation tapes, cassettes, discs, magnetic tapes, hard drives and recordings – to include each document translated, if necessary, through detection devices into reasonably usable form).

J. For purposes of responding to this subpoena, the term "affiliate" shall mean: a corporation, partnership, business trust, joint venture or other artificial entity which effectively controls, or is effectively controlled by you, or which is related to you as parent or subsidiary or sibling entity. "Affiliate" shall also mean any entity in which there is a mutual identity of any officer or director. "Effectively controls" shall mean having the status of owner, investor (if 5% or more of voting stock), partner, member, officer, director, shareholder, manager, settlor, trustee, beneficiary or ultimate equitable owner as defined in Section 607.0505(11)(e), Florida Statutes.

K. The term "Florida affiliates" shall mean those of your affiliates which do business in Florida or which are licensed to do business in Florida.

L. If production of documents or other items required by this subpoena would be, in whole or in part, unduly burdensome, or if the response to an individual request for production may be aided by clarification of the request, contact the Assistant Attorney General who issued this subpoena to discuss possible amendments or modifications of the subpoena, within five (5) days of receipt of same.

M. Unless otherwise specified, the pertinent time period is January 1, YEAR-4 to the present date (hereinafter "pertinent time period") and all questions pertain solely to that narrow time period.

N. Documents maintained in electronic form must be produced in their native electronic form with all metadata intact. Data must be produced in the data format in which it is typically used and maintained. Moreover, to the extent that a responsive Document has been electronically scanned (for any purpose), that Document must be produced in an Optical Character Recognition (OCR) format and an opportunity provided to review the original Document. In addition, documents that have been electronically scanned must be in black and white and should be produced in a Group IV TIFF Format (TIF image format), with a Summation format load file (dii extension). DII Coded data should be received in a **(Comma-Separated Values) CSV format with a pipe (|) used for multivalue fields.** Images should be single page TIFFs, meaning one TIFF file for each page of the Document, not one .tiff for each Document. If there is no text for a text file, the following should be inserted in that text file: "Page Intentionally Left Blank." Moreover, this Subpoena requires all objective coding for the production, to the extent it exists. For electronic mail systems using Microsoft Outlook or LotusNotes, provide all responsive emails and, if applicable, email attachments and any related Documents, in their native file format (i.e., .pst for Outlook personal folder, .nsf for LotusNotes). For all other email systems, provide all responsive emails and, if applicable, email attachments and any related Documents in OCR and TIFF formats as described above.

A party may move under Fed. R. Crim. P. 17(c), to quash a grand jury subpoena on the grounds that it lacks specificity or is burdensome or upon claims of constitutional or common law privilege or Government misconduct or harassment.

Attachment A

1. Organizational charts for Citrus Florida Community Company January 1, YEAR-4 to the present.

2. A copy of the corporate bylaws and articles of incorporation.

3. A copy of all employee manuals from January 1, YEAR-7 to the present.

4. A copy of all Board agendas and minutes from January 1, YEAR-2 to the present.

5. Any and all documents referencing or related to the AOA additive, including, but not limited to:

   a. Any and all press releases or public statements regarding the AOA additive. b. Any and all scientific research regarding the AOA additive.
   c. Any and all marketing research regarding the AOA additive.
   d. Any and all product pricing information or materials for the AOA additive. e. Any and all product placement information or materials regarding the AOA additive.
   f. Any and all product profitability estimates or projections regarding the AOA additive.
   g. Any and all agreements, contracts, or understandings regarding the AOA additive.
   h. Any and all communications (electronic or hard copy) regarding the AOA additive.

6. All documents, materials, and files located at the CFC Research Facility in Gulfport, Florida regarding or related to the AOA additive.

7. A copy of the final AOA test results.

8. A copy of all sales contracts involving orange juice from January 1, YEAR-2 to January 1, YEAR-0.

9. Any and all sales records or data regarding the sale of orange juice containing the AOA additive.

10. Any and all sales records or data regarding the sale of orange juice from September 1, YEAR-2 through February 1, YEAR-1.

11. All purchase records for the sale of orange juice containing the AOA additive.

12. All purchase records for the sale of orange juice from January 1, YEAR-2 to January 1, YEAR-0.

13. Documents sufficient to show Citrus Florida Community Company's total revenue and Profitability (gross and net) from January 1, YEAR-7 to present.

14. Documents sufficient to show Citrus Florida Community Company's total revenue from orange juice sales and profitability (gross and net) from January 1, YEAR-7 to the present.

15. Documents sufficient to show Citrus Florida Community Company's total revenue from orange juice with the AOA additive sales and profitability (gross and net) from January 1, YEAR-7 to the present.

16. All contracts or sales agreements entered into or modified by CFC from January 1, YEAR-4 to the present for the sale of product. This request applies to all product lines distributed by CFC, including, but not limited to, orange juice, cleaning supplies, air fresheners, and other citrus based products.

17. All documents evidencing the amount of product sold by CFC from January 1, YEAR-4 to the present. This request applies to all product lines distributed by CFC, including, but not limited to, orange juice, cleaning supplies, air fresheners, and other citrus based products.

18. All documents evidencing the amount of product shipped to customers from January 1, YEAR-4 to the present and the shipping dates such product was shipped. This request applies to all product lines distributed by CFC, including, but not limited to, orange juice, cleaning supplies, air fresheners, and other citrus based products.

19. The names of all employees responsible for selling product lines for CFC.

20. Copies of all Securities and Exchange Commission filing from January 1, YEAR-4 to the present.

21. Copies of all quarterly revenue statements published or made available to investors, analysts, or the public from January 1, YEAR-4 to the present.

22. All documents provided or made available to investors from January 1, YEAR-2 to the present.

23. Copies of all statements, whether written or verbal, made to investors from January 1, YEAR-2 to the present.

24. All documents regarding or related to CFC's internal investigation of alleged misconduct regarding the use of the AOA additive, including, but not limited to, all documents related to the internal investigation related to the allegations of Logan Walter.

25. All documents within the control of CFC's corporate compliance division regarding the

AOA additive, Ashley Alden, Chris Smart, Jess Henley, Logan Walter, or Sami Myers.

26. All corporate compliance documents or files regarding or mentioning the AOA additive, Ashley Alden, Chris Smart, Jess Henley, Logan Walter, and Sami Myers.

27. A copy of any and all corporate compliance manuals created for CFC and/or any manuals or procedures utilized by CFC's corporate compliance division.

28. All electronic and / or hardcopy calendars, appointment books, diaries, and/or similar documents utilized and maintained by (a) all employees of Citrus Florida Community Company's Product Distribution Division.

29. All documents regarding any "reduction in force" at CFC from January 1, YEAR-4 to the present.

30. All documents regarding and related to the termination of Logan Walter.

31. All e-mails and e-mail attachments sent or received between August 1, YEAR-2 to present by the following individuals regarding the AOA additive, orange juice sales or marketing, any corporate compliance investigation, and/or CFC stock or stock options:

Jody Murray
Kim Vanguard
Cory Campbell
Lynn Smith
Ashley Alden
Chris Smart
Jess Henley
Dr. Sami Myers
Logan Walter

32. The human resources files, employment contracts, performance reviews, reprimands, and payroll records of the following employees:

Jody Murray
Kim Vanguard
Cory Campbell
Lynn Smith
Ashley Alden
Chris Smart
Jess Henley
Dr. Sami Myers
Logan Walter

33. All documents regarding any bonus, stock option, award, or special recognition received by or regarding the following employees:

Jody Murray
Kim Vanguard
Cory Campbell
Lynn Smith
Ashley Alden
Chris Smart
Jess Henley
Dr. Sami Myers
Logan Walter

34. All documents evidencing any sale of CFC stock or shares by the following employees:

Jody Murray
Kim Vanguard
Cory Campbell
Lynn Smith
Ashley Alden
Chris Smart
Jess Henley
Dr. Sami Myers
Logan Walter

35. An electronic copy of the computer hard drives for all company computers used and/or issued to the following employees: Ashley Alden, Chris Smart, Jess Henley, Dr. Sami Myers, and Logan Walter.

36. An electronic copy of the network drives for the following employees: Ashley Alden, Chris Smart, Jess Henley, Dr. Sami Myers, and Logan Walter.

37. An electronic copy of the current and archived email accounts of the following employees: Ashley Alden, Chris Smart, Jess Henley, Dr. Sami Myers, and Logan Walter.

38. Any document or materials produced to another governmental agency, whether local, state, or federal, in response to a document request from January 1, YEAR-2 to the present.

U.S. Department of Justice

The United States Attorney's Office
Tampa, Florida 33601

December 1, YEAR-1

Dear Ashley Alden:

This letter is supplied to a witness scheduled to appear before the federal Grand Jury in order to provide helpful background information about the Grand Jury. The Grand Jury consists of from sixteen to twenty-three persons from the Middle District of Florida. It is their responsibility to inquire into federal crimes which may have been committed in this District.

As a Grand Jury witness you will be asked to testify and answer questions, and to produce records and documents. Only the members of the Grand Jury, attorneys for the United States and a stenographer are permitted in the Grand Jury room while you testify.

We advise you that the Grand Jury is conducting an investigation of possible violations of federal criminal laws involving, but not necessarily limited to fraudulent conduct related to the sale of orange juice containing the AOA additive. You are advised that the destruction or alteration of any document required to be produced before the grand jury or relevant to the grand jury investigation constitutes a serious violation of federal law, including but not limited to Obstruction of Justice.

You are advised that you are a target of the Grand Jury's investigation. You may refuse to answer any question if a truthful answer to the question would tend to incriminate you. Anything that you do or say may be used against you in a subsequent legal proceeding. If you have retained counsel, who represents you personally, the Grand Jury will permit you a reasonable opportunity to step outside the Grand Jury room and confer with counsel if you desire.

Sincerely,

Jo Jones

Jo Jones
Asst. United States Attorney
(222) 111-1111

Attachment M

United States District Court

MIDDLE DISTRICT OF FLORIDA

TO: Ashley Alden
Head, CFC Product Distribution Div.
Tampa, Florida

SUBPOENA TO TESTIFY BEFORE GRAND JURY

SUBPOENA FOR:

☒ PERSON ☒ DOCUMENTS OR OBJECT(S)

YOU ARE HEREBY COMMANDED to appear and testify before the Grand Jury of the United States District Court at the place, date, and time specified below.

PLACE	ROOM
Sam M. Gibbons U.S. Courthouse 801 North Florida Ave. Tampa, Florida 33602	Grand Jury Room
	DATE AND TIME December 15, YEAR-1

YOU ARE ALSO COMMANDED to bring with you the following document(s) or object(s):*

See Attachment A.

☒ *Please see additional information on following page(s)*

This subpoena shall remain in effect until you are granted to leave to depart by the court or by an officer acting on behalf of the court.

CLERK	DATE
Sheryl L. Loesch, Clerk	
(BY) DEPUTY CLERK Thomas Gates	

This subpoena is issued upon application of the United States of America	NAME, ADDRESS AND PHONE NUMBER OF ASSISTANT US ATTORNEY Jo Jones, Assistant United States Attorney 400 North Tampa St., Suite 3200 Tampa, Fl. 33602

* If not applicable, enter "none"

RETURN OF SERVICE [1]

Attachment M

RECEIVED BY SERVER	DATE	PLACE
SERVED	DATE	PLACE

Attachment M

SERVED ON (PRINT NAME)	
SERVED BY (PRINT NAME)	TITLE

STATEMENT OF SERVICE FEES		
TRAVEL	SERVICES	TOTAL

DECLARATION OF SERVER [2]

I declare under penalty of perjury under the laws of the United States of Am erica that the foregoing information contained in the Proof of Service is true and correct.

Executed on ______________________
DATE

____
SIGNATURE OF SERVER

____
ADDRESS OF SERVER

ADDITIONAL INFORMATION

(1) As to who may serve a subpoena and the manner of its service see Rule 17(d), Federal Rules of Criminal Procedure, or Rule 45(c), Federal Rules of Civil Procedure

(2) "Fees and mileage need not be tendered to the witness upon service of a subpoena issues on behalf of the United States or an officer or agency thereof (Rule 45(c), Federal Rules of Civil Procedure) or on behalf of certain indigent parties and criminal defendants who are unable to pay such costs (28 USC 1825, Rule 17(b) Federal Rules of Criminal Procedure)".

Attachment M

DEFINITIONS AND INSTRUCTIONS

A. "You" or "Your" as used herein means any of the respondents, their agents and employees or any "affiliate" of the aforementioned entities, as that term is herein defined.

Your agents include but are not limited to your officers, directors, attorneys, accountants, CPA's, advertising consultants, or advertising account representatives.

Any document in the possession of you, your affiliates, your agents or your employees is deemed to be within your possession or control. You have the affirmative duty to contact your agents, affiliates and employees and to obtain documentation from them, if such documentation is responsive to this subpoena.

B. Unless otherwise indicated, documents to be produced pursuant to this subpoena should include all original documents prepared, sent, dated, received, in effect, or which otherwise came into existence at any time. If your "original" is a photocopy, then the photocopy would be and should be produced as the original.

C. This subpoena duces tecum calls for the production of all responsive documents in your possession, custody or control without regard to the physical location of said documents.

D. "And" and "or" are used as terms of inclusion, not exclusion.

E. The documents to be produced pursuant to each request should be segregated and specifically identified to indicate clearly the particular numbered request to which they are responsive.

F. In the event that you seek to withhold any document on the basis that is properly entitled to some privilege or limitation, please provide the following information:

1. A list identifying each document for which you believe a limitation exists;
2. The name of each author, writer, sender or initiator of such document or thing, if any;
3. The name of each recipient, addressee or party for whom such document or thing was intended, if any;
4. The date of such document, if any, or an estimate thereof so indicated if no date appears on the document;
5. The general subject matter as described in such document, or, if no such description appears, then such other description sufficient to identify said document; and
6. The claimed grounds for withholding the document, including, but not limited to, the nature of any claimed privilege and grounds in support thereof.

G. For each request, or part thereof, which is not fully responded to pursuant to a privilege, the nature of the privilege and grounds in support thereof should be fully stated.

H. If you possess, control or have custody of no documents responsive to any of the numbered requests set forth below, state this fact in your response to said request.

I. For purposes of responding to this subpoena, the term "document" shall mean all writings or stored data or information of any kind, in any form, including the originals and all non-identical copies, whether different from the originals by reason of any notation(s) made on such copies or otherwise, including, without limitation: correspondence, notes, letters, telegrams, minutes, certificates, diplomas, contracts, franchise agreements and other agreements, brochures, pamphlets, forms, scripts, reports, studies, statistics, inter-office and intra-office communications, training materials, analyses, memoranda,

statements, summaries, graphs, charts, tests, plans, arrangements, tabulations, bulletins, newsletters, advertisements, computer printouts, teletype, telefax, microfilm, e-mail, electronically stored data, price books and lists, invoices, receipts, inventories, regularly kept summaries or compilations of business records, notations of any type of conversations, meetings, telephone or other communications, audio and videotapes; electronic, mechanical or electrical records or representations of any kind (including without limitation tapes, cassettes, discs, magnetic tapes, hard drives and recordings – to include each document translated, if necessary, through detection devices into reasonably usable form).

J. For purposes of responding to this subpoena, the term "affiliate" shall mean: a corporation, partnership, business trust, joint venture or other artificial entity which effectively controls, or is effectively controlled by you, or which is related to you as parent or subsidiary or sibling entity. "Affiliate" shall also mean any entity in which there is a mutual identity of any officer or director. "Effectively controls" shall mean having the status of owner, investor (if 5% or more of voting stock), partner, member, officer, director, shareholder, manager, settlor, trustee, beneficiary or ultimate equitable owner as defined in Section 607.0505(11)(e), Florida Statutes.

K. The term "Florida affiliates" shall mean those of your affiliates which do business in Florida or which are licensed to do business in Florida.

L. If production of documents or other items required by this subpoena would be, in whole or in part, unduly burdensome, or if the response to an individual request for production may be aided by clarification of the request, contact the Assistant Attorney General who issued this subpoena to discuss possible amendments or modifications of the subpoena, within five (5) days of receipt of same.

M. Unless otherwise specified, the pertinent time period is January 1, YEAR-4 to the present date (hereinafter "pertinent time period") and all questions pertain solely to that narrow time period.

N. Documents maintained in electronic form must be produced in their native electronic form with all metadata intact. Data must be produced in the data format in which it is typically used and maintained. Moreover, to the extent that a responsive Document has been electronically scanned (for any purpose), that Document must be produced in an Optical Character Recognition (OCR) format and an opportunity provided to review the original Document. In addition, documents that have been electronically scanned must be in black and white and should be produced in a Group IV TIFF Format (TIF image format), with a Summation format load file (dii extension). DII Coded data should be received in a **(Comma-Separated Values) CSV format with a pipe (|) used for multivalue fields.** Images should be single page TIFFs, meaning one TIFF file for each page of the Document, not one .tiff for each Document. If there is no text for a text file, the following should be inserted in that text file: "Page Intentionally Left Blank." Moreover, this Subpoena requires all objective coding for the production, to the extent it exists. For electronic mail systems using Microsoft Outlook or LotusNotes, provide all responsive emails and, if applicable, email attachments and any related Documents, in their native file format (i.e., .pst for Outlook personal folder, .nsf for LotusNotes). For all other email systems, provide all responsive emails and, if applicable, email attachments and any related Documents in OCR and TIFF formats as described above.

A party may move under Fed. R. Crim. P. 17(c), to quash a grand jury subpoena on the grounds that it lacks specificity or is burdensome or upon claims of constitutional or common law privilege or Government misconduct or harassment.

Attachment A

1. Any and all documents referencing or related to the AOA additive.
2. Any and all communications, including email and letter communications, referencing or related to the AOA additive.
3. Any and all pay stubs received from the Citrus Florida Community Company.
4. Any and all documents referencing or regarding your receipt of an award of stock options or a bonus by the Citrus Florida Community Company.
5. Any and all documents referencing or regarding your exercise of stock options in the Citrus Florida Community Company's stock/shares.
6. Any and all documents referencing or regarding your sale of Citrus Florida Community Company stock/shares.
7. Copies of all bank account statements from any personal bank account held in your name, even if in combination with others, for the last ten years.
8. Any and all documents referencing or regarding any corporate compliance investigation conducted the Citrus Florida Community Company regarding or related to the AOA additive.
9. All diaries, calendars, or notebooks containing any information regarding the Central Florida Company.

U.S. Department of Justice

The United States Attorney's Office
Tampa, Florida 33601

December 1, YEAR-1

Dear Chris Smart:

This letter is supplied to a witness scheduled to appear before the federal Grand Jury in order to provide helpful background information about the Grand Jury. The Grand Jury consists of from sixteen to twenty-three persons from the Middle District of Florida. It is their responsibility to inquire into federal crimes which may have been committed in this District.

As a Grand Jury witness you will be asked to testify and answer questions, and to produce records and documents. Only the members of the Grand Jury, attorneys for the United States and a stenographer are permitted in the Grand Jury room while you testify.

We advise you that the Grand Jury is conducting an investigation of possible violations of federal criminal laws involving, but not necessarily limited to fraudulent conduct related to the sale of orange juice containing the AOA additive. You are advised that the destruction or alteration of any document required to be produced before the grand jury or relevant to the grand jury investigation constitutes a serious violation of federal law, including but not limited to Obstruction of Justice.

You are advised that you are a target of the Grand Jury's investigation. You may refuse to answer any question if a truthful answer to the question would tend to incriminate you. Anything that you do or say may be used against you in a subsequent legal proceeding. If you have retained counsel, who represents you personally, the Grand Jury will permit you a reasonable opportunity to step outside the Grand Jury room and confer with counsel if you desire.

Sincerely,

Jo Jones

Jo Jones
Asst. United States Attorney
(222) 111-1111

Attachment M

United States District Court

MIDDLE **DISTRICT OF** FLORIDA

TO: Chris Smart
CFC Marketing Team
Tampa, Florida

SUBPOENA TO TESTIFY BEFORE GRAND JURY

SUBPOENA FOR:

☒ PERSON ☒ DOCUMENTS OR OBJECT(S)

YOU ARE HEREBY COMMANDED to appear and testify before the Grand Jury of the United States District Court at the place, date, and time specified below.

PLACE	ROOM
Sam M. Gibbons U.S. Courthouse 801 North Florida Ave. Tampa, Florida 33602	Grand Jury Room DATE AND TIME December 15, YEAR-1

YOU ARE ALSO COMMANDED to bring with you the following document(s) or object(s):*

See Attachment A.

☒ *Please see additional information on following page(s)*

This subpoena shall remain in effect until you are granted to leave to depart by the court or by an officer acting on behalf of the court.

CLERK	DATE
Sheryl L. Loesch, Clerk	
(BY) DEPUTY CLERK Thomas Gates	

UNITED STATES DISTRICT COURT * MIDDLE DISTRICT OF FLORIDA

This subpoena is issued upon application of the United States of America	NAME, ADDRESS AND PHONE NUMBER OF ASSISTANT US ATTORNEY Jo Jones, Assistant United States Attorney 400 North Tampa St., Suite 3200 Tampa, Fl. 33602

* If not applicable, enter "none"

RETURN OF SERVICE (1)

Attachment M

RECEIVED BY SERVER	DATE	PLACE
SERVED	DATE	PLACE

Attachment M

SERVED ON (PRINT NAME)	
SERVED BY (PRINT NAME)	TITLE

STATEMENT OF SERVICE FEES

TRAVEL	SERVICES	TOTAL

DECLARATION OF SERVER [(2)]

I declare under penalty of perjury under the laws of the United States of Am erica that the foregoing information contained in the Proof of Service is true and correct.

Executed on ____________________ DATE ____________________ SIGNATURE OF SERVER

____________________ ADDRESS OF SERVER

____

ADDITIONAL INFORMATION

(1) As to who may serve a subpoena and the manner of its service see Rule 17(d), Federal Rules of Criminal Procedure, or Rule 45(c), Federal Rules of Civil Procedure

(2) "Fees and mileage need not be tendered to the witness upon service of a subpoena issues on behalf of the United States or an officer or agency thereof (Rule 45(c), Federal Rules of Civil Procedure) or on behalf of certain indigent parties and criminal defendants who are unable to pay such costs (28 USC 1825, Rule 17(b) Federal Rules of Criminal Procedure)".

Attachment M

DEFINITIONS AND INSTRUCTIONS

A. "You" or "Your" as used herein means any of the respondents, their agents and employees or any "affiliate" of the aforementioned entities, as that term is herein defined.

Your agents include but are not limited to your officers, directors, attorneys, accountants, CPA's, advertising consultants, or advertising account representatives.

Any document in the possession of you, your affiliates, your agents or your employees is deemed to be within your possession or control. You have the affirmative duty to contact your agents, affiliates and employees and to obtain documentation from them, if such documentation is responsive to this subpoena.

B. Unless otherwise indicated, documents to be produced pursuant to this subpoena should include all original documents prepared, sent, dated, received, in effect, or which otherwise came into existence at any time. If your "original" is a photocopy, then the photocopy would be and should be produced as the original.

C. This subpoena duces tecum calls for the production of all responsive documents in your possession, custody or control without regard to the physical location of said documents.

D. "And" and "or" are used as terms of inclusion, not exclusion.

E. The documents to be produced pursuant to each request should be segregated and specifically identified to indicate clearly the particular numbered request to which they are responsive.

F. In the event that you seek to withhold any document on the basis that is properly entitled to some privilege or limitation, please provide the following information:

1. A list identifying each document for which you believe a limitation exists;
2. The name of each author, writer, sender or initiator of such document or thing, if any;
3. The name of each recipient, addressee or party for whom such document or thing was intended, if any;
4. The date of such document, if any, or an estimate thereof so indicated if no date appears on the document;
5. The general subject matter as described in such document, or, if no such description appears, then such other description sufficient to identify said document; and
6. The claimed grounds for withholding the document, including, but not limited to, the nature of any claimed privilege and grounds in support thereof.

G. For each request, or part thereof, which is not fully responded to pursuant to a privilege, the nature of the privilege and grounds in support thereof should be fully stated.

H. If you possess, control or have custody of no documents responsive to any of the numbered requests set forth below, state this fact in your response to said request.

I. For purposes of responding to this subpoena, the term "document" shall mean all writings or stored data or information of any kind, in any form, including the originals and all non-identical copies, whether different from the originals by reason of any notation(s) made on such copies or otherwise, including, without limitation: correspondence, notes, letters, telegrams, minutes, certificates, diplomas, contracts, franchise agreements and other agreements, brochures, pamphlets, forms, scripts, reports, studies, statistics, inter-office and intra-office communications, training materials, analyses, memoranda,

statements, summaries, graphs, charts, tests, plans, arrangements, tabulations, bulletins, newsletters, advertisements, computer printouts, teletype, telefax, microfilm, e-mail, electronically stored data, price books and lists, invoices, receipts, inventories, regularly kept summaries or compilations of business records, notations of any type of conversations, meetings, telephone or other communications, audio and videotapes; electronic, mechanical or electrical records or representations of any kind (including without limitation tapes, cassettes, discs, magnetic tapes, hard drives and recordings – to include each document translated, if necessary, through detection devices into reasonably usable form).

J. For purposes of responding to this subpoena, the term "affiliate" shall mean: a corporation, partnership, business trust, joint venture or other artificial entity which effectively controls, or is effectively controlled by you, or which is related to you as parent or subsidiary or sibling entity. "Affiliate" shall also mean any entity in which there is a mutual identity of any officer or director. "Effectively controls" shall mean having the status of owner, investor (if 5% or more of voting stock), partner, member, officer, director, shareholder, manager, settlor, trustee, beneficiary or ultimate equitable owner as defined in Section 607.0505(11)(e), Florida Statutes.

K. The term "Florida affiliates" shall mean those of your affiliates which do business in Florida or which are licensed to do business in Florida.

L. If production of documents or other items required by this subpoena would be, in whole or in part, unduly burdensome, or if the response to an individual request for production may be aided by clarification of the request, contact the Assistant Attorney General who issued this subpoena to discuss possible amendments or modifications of the subpoena, within five (5) days of receipt of same.

M. Unless otherwise specified, the pertinent time period is January 1, YEAR-4 to the present date (hereinafter "pertinent time period") and all questions pertain solely to that narrow time period.

N. Documents maintained in electronic form must be produced in their native electronic form with all metadata intact. Data must be produced in the data format in which it is typically used and maintained. Moreover, to the extent that a responsive Document has been electronically scanned (for any purpose), that Document must be produced in an Optical Character Recognition (OCR) format and an opportunity provided to review the original Document. In addition, documents that have been electronically scanned must be in black and white and should be produced in a Group IV TIFF Format (TIF image format), with a Summation format load file (dii extension). DII Coded data should be received in a **(Comma-Separated Values) CSV format with a pipe (|) used for multivalue fields.** Images should be single page TIFFs, meaning one TIFF file for each page of the Document, not one .tiff for each Document. If there is no text for a text file, the following should be inserted in that text file: "Page Intentionally Left Blank." Moreover, this Subpoena requires all objective coding for the production, to the extent it exists. For electronic mail systems using Microsoft Outlook or LotusNotes, provide all responsive emails and, if applicable, email attachments and any related Documents, in their native file format (i.e., .pst for Outlook personal folder, .nsf for LotusNotes). For all other email systems, provide all responsive emails and, if applicable, email attachments and any related Documents in OCR and TIFF formats as described above.

A party may move under Fed. R. Crim. P. 17(c), to quash a grand jury subpoena on the grounds that it lacks specificity or is burdensome or upon claims of constitutional or common law privilege or Government misconduct or harassment.

Attachment A

1. Any and all documents referencing or related to the AOA additive.
2. Any and all communications, including email and letter communications, referencing or related to the AOA additive.
3. Any and all pay stubs received from the Citrus Florida Community Company.
4. Any and all documents referencing or regarding your receipt of an award of stock options or a bonus by the Citrus Florida Community Company.
5. Any and all documents referencing or regarding your exercise of stock options in the Citrus Florida Community Company's stock/shares.
6. Any and all documents referencing or regarding your sale of Citrus Florida Community Company stock/shares.
7. Copies of all bank account statements from any personal bank account held in your name, even if in combination with others, for the last ten years.
8. Any and all documents referencing or regarding any corporate compliance investigation conducted the Citrus Florida Community Company regarding or related to the AOA additive.
9. All diaries, calendars, or notebooks containing any information regarding the Central Florida Company.

U.S. Department of Justice

The United States Attorney's Office
Tampa, Florida 33601

December 1, YEAR-1

Dear Jess Henley:

This letter is supplied to a witness scheduled to appear before the federal Grand Jury in order to provide helpful background information about the Grand Jury. The Grand Jury consists of from sixteen to twenty-three persons from the Middle District of Florida. It is their responsibility to inquire into federal crimes which may have been committed in this District.

As a Grand Jury witness you will be asked to testify and answer questions, and to produce records and documents. Only the members of the Grand Jury, attorneys for the United States and a stenographer are permitted in the Grand Jury room while you testify.

We advise you that the Grand Jury is conducting an investigation of possible violations of federal criminal laws involving, but not necessarily limited to fraudulent conduct related to the sale of orange juice containing the AOA additive. You are advised that the destruction or alteration of any document required to be produced before the grand jury or relevant to the grand jury investigation constitutes a serious violation of federal law, including but not limited to Obstruction of Justice.

You are advised that you are a target of the Grand Jury's investigation. You may refuse to answer any question if a truthful answer to the question would tend to incriminate you. Anything that you do or say may be used against you in a subsequent legal proceeding. If you have retained counsel, who represents you personally, the Grand Jury will permit you a reasonable opportunity to step outside the Grand Jury room and confer with counsel if you desire.

Sincerely,

Jo Jones

Jo Jones
Asst. United States Attorney
(222) 111-1111

Attachment M

United States District Court

MIDDLE DISTRICT OF FLORIDA

TO: Jess Henley
CFC Sales Team
Tampa, Florida

SUBPOENA TO TESTIFY BEFORE GRAND JURY

SUBPOENA FOR:

☒ PERSON ☒ DOCUMENTS OR OBJECT(S)

YOU ARE HEREBY COMMANDED to appear and testify before the Grand Jury of the United States District Court at the place, date, and time specified below.

PLACE	ROOM
Sam M. Gibbons U.S. Courthouse 801 North Florida Ave. Tampa, Florida 33602	Grand Jury Room
	DATE AND TIME December 15, YEAR-1

YOU ARE ALSO COMMANDED to bring with you the following document(s) or object(s):*

See Attachment A.

☒ *Please see additional information on following page(s)*

This subpoena shall remain in effect until you are granted to leave to depart by the court or by an officer acting on behalf of the court.

CLERK	DATE
Sheryl L. Loesch, Clerk	
(BY) DEPUTY CLERK Thomas Gates	

	NAME, ADDRESS AND PHONE NUMBER OF ASSISTANT US ATTORNEY
This subpoena is issued upon application of the United States of America	Jo Jones, Assistant United States Attorney 400 North Tampa St., Suite 3200 Tampa, Fl. 33602

UNITED STATES DISTRICT COURT
MIDDLE DISTRICT OF FLORIDA

* If not applicable, enter "none"

RETURN OF SERVICE [1]

Attachment M

RECEIVED BY SERVER	DATE	PLACE
SERVED	DATE	PLACE

Attachment M

SERVED ON (PRINT NAME)		
SERVED BY (PRINT NAME)		TITLE

STATEMENT OF SERVICE FEES		
TRAVEL	SERVICES	TOTAL

DECLARATION OF SERVER [2]

I declare under penalty of perjury under the laws of the United States of Am erica that the foregoing information contained in the Proof of Service is true and correct.

Executed on ____________________
DATE

____
SIGNATURE OF SERVER

____
ADDRESS OF SERVER

____

ADDITIONAL INFORMATION

(1) As to who may serve a subpoena and the manner of its service see Rule 17(d), Federal Rules of Criminal Procedure, or Rule 45(c), Federal Rules of Civil Procedure

(2) "Fees and mileage need not be tendered to the witness upon service of a subpoena issues on behalf of the United States or an officer or agency thereof (Rule 45(c), Federal Rules of Civil Procedure) or on behalf of certain indigent parties and criminal defendants who are unable to pay such costs (28 USC 1825, Rule 17(b) Federal Rules of Criminal Procedure)".

DEFINITIONS AND INSTRUCTIONS

A. "You" or "Your" as used herein means any of the respondents, their agents and employees or any "affiliate" of the aforementioned entities, as that term is herein defined.

Your agents include but are not limited to your officers, directors, attorneys, accountants, CPA's, advertising consultants, or advertising account representatives.

Any document in the possession of you, your affiliates, your agents or your employees is deemed to be within your possession or control. You have the affirmative duty to contact your agents, affiliates and employees and to obtain documentation from them, if such documentation is responsive to this subpoena.

B. Unless otherwise indicated, documents to be produced pursuant to this subpoena should include all original documents prepared, sent, dated, received, in effect, or which otherwise came into existence at any time. If your "original" is a photocopy, then the photocopy would be and should be produced as the original.

C. This subpoena duces tecum calls for the production of all responsive documents in your possession, custody or control without regard to the physical location of said documents.

D. "And" and "or" are used as terms of inclusion, not exclusion.

E. The documents to be produced pursuant to each request should be segregated and specifically identified to indicate clearly the particular numbered request to which they are responsive.

F. In the event that you seek to withhold any document on the basis that is properly entitled to some privilege or limitation, please provide the following information:

1. A list identifying each document for which you believe a limitation exists;
2. The name of each author, writer, sender or initiator of such document or thing, if any;
3. The name of each recipient, addressee or party for whom such document or thing was intended, if any;
4. The date of such document, if any, or an estimate thereof so indicated if no date appears on the document;
5. The general subject matter as described in such document, or, if no such description appears, then such other description sufficient to identify said document; and
6. The claimed grounds for withholding the document, including, but not limited to, the nature of any claimed privilege and grounds in support thereof.

G. For each request, or part thereof, which is not fully responded to pursuant to a privilege, the nature of the privilege and grounds in support thereof should be fully stated.

H. If you possess, control or have custody of no documents responsive to any of the numbered requests set forth below, state this fact in your response to said request.

I. For purposes of responding to this subpoena, the term "document" shall mean all writings or stored data or information of any kind, in any form, including the originals and all non-identical copies, whether different from the originals by reason of any notation(s) made on such copies or otherwise, including, without limitation: correspondence, notes, letters, telegrams, minutes, certificates, diplomas, contracts, franchise agreements and other agreements, brochures, pamphlets, forms, scripts, reports, studies, statistics, inter-office and intra-office communications, training materials, analyses, memoranda,

statements, summaries, graphs, charts, tests, plans, arrangements, tabulations, bulletins, newsletters, advertisements, computer printouts, teletype, telefax, microfilm, e-mail, electronically stored data, price books and lists, invoices, receipts, inventories, regularly kept summaries or compilations of business records, notations of any type of conversations, meetings, telephone or other communications, audio and videotapes; electronic, mechanical or electrical records or representations of any kind (including without limitation tapes, cassettes, discs, magnetic tapes, hard drives and recordings – to include each document translated, if necessary, through detection devices into reasonably usable form).

J. For purposes of responding to this subpoena, the term "affiliate" shall mean: a corporation, partnership, business trust, joint venture or other artificial entity which effectively controls, or is effectively controlled by you, or which is related to you as parent or subsidiary or sibling entity. "Affiliate" shall also mean any entity in which there is a mutual identity of any officer or director. "Effectively controls" shall mean having the status of owner, investor (if 5% or more of voting stock), partner, member, officer, director, shareholder, manager, settlor, trustee, beneficiary or ultimate equitable owner as defined in Section 607.0505(11)(e), Florida Statutes.

K. The term "Florida affiliates" shall mean those of your affiliates which do business in Florida or which are licensed to do business in Florida.

L. If production of documents or other items required by this subpoena would be, in whole or in part, unduly burdensome, or if the response to an individual request for production may be aided by clarification of the request, contact the Assistant Attorney General who issued this subpoena to discuss possible amendments or modifications of the subpoena, within five (5) days of receipt of same.

M. Unless otherwise specified, the pertinent time period is January 1, YEAR-4 to the present date (hereinafter "pertinent time period") and all questions pertain solely to that narrow time period.

N. Documents maintained in electronic form must be produced in their native electronic form with all metadata intact. Data must be produced in the data format in which it is typically used and maintained. Moreover, to the extent that a responsive Document has been electronically scanned (for any purpose), that Document must be produced in an Optical Character Recognition (OCR) format and an opportunity provided to review the original Document. In addition, documents that have been electronically scanned must be in black and white and should be produced in a Group IV TIFF Format (TIF image format), with a Summation format load file (dii extension). DII Coded data should be received in a **(Comma-Separated Values) CSV format with a pipe (|) used for multivalue fields.** Images should be single page TIFFs, meaning one TIFF file for each page of the Document, not one .tiff for each Document. If there is no text for a text file, the following should be inserted in that text file: "Page Intentionally Left Blank." Moreover, this Subpoena requires all objective coding for the production, to the extent it exists. For electronic mail systems using Microsoft Outlook or LotusNotes, provide all responsive emails and, if applicable, email attachments and any related Documents, in their native file format (i.e., .pst for Outlook personal folder, .nsf for LotusNotes). For all other email systems, provide all responsive emails and, if applicable, email attachments and any related Documents in OCR and TIFF formats as described above.

A party may move under Fed. R. Crim. P. 17(c), to quash a grand jury subpoena on the grounds that it lacks specificity or is burdensome or upon claims of constitutional or common law privilege or Government misconduct or harassment.

Attachment A

1. Any and all documents referencing or related to the AOA additive.
2. Any and all communications, including email and letter communications, referencing or related to the AOA additive.
3. Any and all pay stubs received from the Citrus Florida Community Company.
4. Any and all documents referencing or regarding your receipt of an award of stock options or a bonus by the Citrus Florida Community Company.
5. Any and all documents referencing or regarding your exercise of stock options in the Citrus Florida Community Company's stock/shares.
6. Any and all documents referencing or regarding your sale of Citrus Florida Community Company stock/shares.
7. Copies of all bank account statements from any personal bank account held in your name, even if in combination with others, for the last ten years.
8. Any and all documents referencing or regarding any corporate compliance investigation conducted the Citrus Florida Community Company regarding or related to the AOA additive.
9. All diaries, calendars, or notebooks containing any information regarding the Central Florida Company.

U.S. Department of Justice

The United States Attorney's Office
Tampa, Florida 33601

December 1, YEAR-1

Dear Sami Myers:

This letter is supplied to a witness scheduled to appear before the federal Grand Jury in order to provide helpful background information about the Grand Jury. The Grand Jury consists of from sixteen to twenty-three persons from the Middle District of Florida. It is their responsibility to inquire into federal crimes which may have been committed in this District.

As a Grand Jury witness you will be asked to testify and answer questions, and to produce records and documents. Only the members of the Grand Jury, attorneys for the United States and a stenographer are permitted in the Grand Jury room while you testify.

We advise you that the Grand Jury is conducting an investigation of possible violations of federal criminal laws involving, but not necessarily limited to fraudulent conduct related to the sale of orange juice containing the AOA additive. You are advised that the destruction or alteration of any document required to be produced before the grand jury or relevant to the grand jury investigation constitutes a serious violation of federal law, including but not limited to Obstruction of Justice.

You are advised that you are a target of the Grand Jury's investigation. You may refuse to answer any question if a truthful answer to the question would tend to incriminate you. Anything that you do or say may be used against you in a subsequent legal proceeding. If you have retained counsel, who represents you personally, the Grand Jury will permit you a reasonable opportunity to step outside the Grand Jury room and confer with counsel if you desire.

Sincerely,

Jo Jones

Jo Jones
Asst. United States Attorney
(222) 111-1111

Attachment M

United States District Court

MIDDLE	DISTRICT OF	FLORIDA

TO: Sami Myers
Head, CFC Research Facility
Gulfport, Florida

SUBPOENA TO TESTIFY BEFORE GRAND JURY

SUBPOENA FOR:

☒ PERSON ☒ DOCUMENTS OR OBJECT(S)

YOU ARE HEREBY COMMANDED to appear and testify before the Grand Jury of the United States District Court at the place, date, and time specified below.

PLACE	ROOM
Sam M. Gibbons U.S. Courthouse 801 North Florida Ave. Tampa, Florida 33602	Grand Jury Room DATE AND TIME December 15, YEAR-1

YOU ARE ALSO COMMANDED to bring with you the following document(s) or object(s):*

<u>See</u> Attachment A.

☒ *Please see additional information on following page(s)*

This subpoena shall remain in effect until you are granted to leave to depart by the court or by an officer acting on behalf of the court.

CLERK	DATE
Sheryl L. Loesch, Clerk	
(BY) DEPUTY CLERK Thomas Gates	

This subpoena is issued upon application of the United States of America	NAME, ADDRESS AND PHONE NUMBER OF ASSISTANT US ATTORNEY Jo Jones, Assistant United States Attorney 400 North Tampa St., Suite 3200 Tampa, Fl. 33602

* If not applicable, enter "none"

RETURN OF SERVICE [(1)]

Attachment M

RECEIVED BY SERVER	DATE	PLACE
SERVED	DATE	PLACE

Attachment M

SERVED ON (PRINT NAME)		
SERVED BY (PRINT NAME)		TITLE
STATEMENT OF SERVICE FEES		
TRAVEL	SERVICES	TOTAL

DECLARATION OF SERVER [(2)]

I declare under penalty of perjury under the laws of the United States of Am erica that the foregoing information contained in the Proof of Service is true and correct.

Executed on ______________________ ______________________

DATE SIGNATURE OF SERVER

____

ADDRESS OF SERVER

____

ADDITIONAL INFORMATION

(1) As to who may serve a subpoena and the manner of its service see Rule 17(d), Federal Rules of Criminal Procedure, or Rule 45(c), Federal Rules of Civil Procedure

(2) "Fees and mileage need not be tendered to the witness upon service of a subpoena issues on behalf of the United States or an officer or agency thereof (Rule 45(c), Federal Rules of Civil Procedure) or on behalf of certain indigent parties and criminal defendants who are unable to pay such costs (28 USC 1825, Rule 17(b) Federal Rules of Criminal Procedure)".

Attachment M

DEFINITIONS AND INSTRUCTIONS

A. "You" or "Your" as used herein means any of the respondents, their agents and employees or any "affiliate" of the aforementioned entities, as that term is herein defined.

Your agents include but are not limited to your officers, directors, attorneys, accountants, CPA's, advertising consultants, or advertising account representatives.

Any document in the possession of you, your affiliates, your agents or your employees is deemed to be within your possession or control. You have the affirmative duty to contact your agents, affiliates and employees and to obtain documentation from them, if such documentation is responsive to this subpoena.

B. Unless otherwise indicated, documents to be produced pursuant to this subpoena should include all original documents prepared, sent, dated, received, in effect, or which otherwise came into existence at any time. If your "original" is a photocopy, then the photocopy would be and should be produced as the original.

C. This subpoena duces tecum calls for the production of all responsive documents in your possession, custody or control without regard to the physical location of said documents.

D. "And" and "or" are used as terms of inclusion, not exclusion.

E. The documents to be produced pursuant to each request should be segregated and specifically identified to indicate clearly the particular numbered request to which they are responsive.

F. In the event that you seek to withhold any document on the basis that is properly entitled to some privilege or limitation, please provide the following information:

1. A list identifying each document for which you believe a limitation exists;
2. The name of each author, writer, sender or initiator of such document or thing, if any;
3. The name of each recipient, addressee or party for whom such document or thing was intended, if any;
4. The date of such document, if any, or an estimate thereof so indicated if no date appears on the document;
5. The general subject matter as described in such document, or, if no such description appears, then such other description sufficient to identify said document; and
6. The claimed grounds for withholding the document, including, but not limited to, the nature of any claimed privilege and grounds in support thereof.

G. For each request, or part thereof, which is not fully responded to pursuant to a privilege, the nature of the privilege and grounds in support thereof should be fully stated.

H. If you possess, control or have custody of no documents responsive to any of the numbered requests set forth below, state this fact in your response to said request.

I. For purposes of responding to this subpoena, the term "document" shall mean all writings or stored data or information of any kind, in any form, including the originals and all non-identical copies, whether different from the originals by reason of any notation(s) made on such copies or otherwise, including, without limitation: correspondence, notes, letters, telegrams, minutes, certificates, diplomas, contracts, franchise agreements and other agreements, brochures, pamphlets, forms, scripts, reports, studies, statistics, inter-office and intra-office communications, training materials, analyses, memoranda,

statements, summaries, graphs, charts, tests, plans, arrangements, tabulations, bulletins, newsletters, advertisements, computer printouts, teletype, telefax, microfilm, e-mail, electronically stored data, price books and lists, invoices, receipts, inventories, regularly kept summaries or compilations of business records, notations of any type of conversations, meetings, telephone or other communications, audio and videotapes; electronic, mechanical or electrical records or representations of any kind (including without limitation tapes, cassettes, discs, magnetic tapes, hard drives and recordings – to include each document translated, if necessary, through detection devices into reasonably usable form).

J. For purposes of responding to this subpoena, the term "affiliate" shall mean: a corporation, partnership, business trust, joint venture or other artificial entity which effectively controls, or is effectively controlled by you, or which is related to you as parent or subsidiary or sibling entity. "Affiliate" shall also mean any entity in which there is a mutual identity of any officer or director. "Effectively controls" shall mean having the status of owner, investor (if 5% or more of voting stock), partner, member, officer, director, shareholder, manager, settlor, trustee, beneficiary or ultimate equitable owner as defined in Section 607.0505(11)(e), Florida Statutes.

K. The term "Florida affiliates" shall mean those of your affiliates which do business in Florida or which are licensed to do business in Florida.

L. If production of documents or other items required by this subpoena would be, in whole or in part, unduly burdensome, or if the response to an individual request for production may be aided by clarification of the request, contact the Assistant Attorney General who issued this subpoena to discuss possible amendments or modifications of the subpoena, within five (5) days of receipt of same.

M. Unless otherwise specified, the pertinent time period is January 1, YEAR-4 to the present date (hereinafter "pertinent time period") and all questions pertain solely to that narrow time period.

N. Documents maintained in electronic form must be produced in their native electronic form with all metadata intact. Data must be produced in the data format in which it is typically used and maintained. Moreover, to the extent that a responsive Document has been electronically scanned (for any purpose), that Document must be produced in an Optical Character Recognition (OCR) format and an opportunity provided to review the original Document. In addition, documents that have been electronically scanned must be in black and white and should be produced in a Group IV TIFF Format (TIF image format), with a Summation format load file (dii extension). DII Coded data should be received in a **(Comma-Separated Values) CSV format with a pipe (|) used for multivalue fields.** Images should be single page TIFFs, meaning one TIFF file for each page of the Document, not one .tiff for each Document. If there is no text for a text file, the following should be inserted in that text file: "Page Intentionally Left Blank." Moreover, this Subpoena requires all objective coding for the production, to the extent it exists. For electronic mail systems using Microsoft Outlook or LotusNotes, provide all responsive emails and, if applicable, email attachments and any related Documents, in their native file format (i.e., .pst for Outlook personal folder, .nsf for LotusNotes). For all other email systems, provide all responsive emails and, if applicable, email attachments and any related Documents in OCR and TIFF formats as described above.

A party may move under Fed. R. Crim. P. 17(c), to quash a grand jury subpoena on the grounds that it lacks specificity or is burdensome or upon claims of constitutional or common law privilege or Government misconduct or harassment.

Attachment A

1. Any and all documents referencing or related to the AOA additive.
2. Any and all communications, including email and letter communications, referencing or related to the AOA additive.
3. Any and all pay stubs received from the Citrus Florida Community Company.
4. Any and all documents referencing or regarding your receipt of an award of stock options or a bonus by the Citrus Florida Community Company.
5. Any and all documents referencing or regarding your exercise of stock options in the Citrus Florida Community Company's stock/shares.
6. Any and all documents referencing or regarding your sale of Citrus Florida Community Company stock/shares.
7. Copies of all bank account statements from any personal bank account held in your name, even if in combination with others, for the last ten years.
8. Any and all documents referencing or regarding any corporate compliance investigation conducted the Citrus Florida Community Company regarding or related to the AOA additive.
9. All diaries, calendars, or notebooks containing any information regarding the Central Florida Company.

STATE OF FLORIDA
IN THE CIRCUIT COURT FOR THE THIRTEENTH JUDICIAL CIRCUIT
IN AND FOR HILLSBOROUGH COUNTY, FLORIDA

LOGAN WALTER	)
	)
Plaintiff,	)
	)
vs.	)
	)
CITRUS FLORIDA COMMUNITY COMPANY, a Florida Corporation, ASHLEY ALDEN, CHRIS SMART, JESS HENLEY, SAMI MYERS, and LYNN SMITH	)
	)
Defendants.	)
	)

PLAINTIFF'S FIRST REQUEST FOR PRODUCTION TO DEFENDANTS

Plaintiff, by and through his/her undersigned counsel, hereby gives notice to Defendants, Citrus Florida Community Company ("CFC"), Ashley Alden, Chris Smart, Jess Henley, and Sami Myers, to produce for the purpose of inspection and copying at the law offices of Plaintiff Law LLP within thirty (30) days of service hereof, the following documents, papers, and things.

INSTRUCTIONS

A. To the extent that a claim of privilege is made for any requested documents, identify the privilege and each document to which it would apply.

B. If any of the documents cannot be produced in full, produce to the extent possible, specifying the specific reasons for the inability to produce the remainder.

C. If any document has been destroyed or no longer exists for any reason, state the disposition of that document, when and by whom it was disposed, and the reason for its disposition.

Attachment N

D. This request for production should be deemed continuing in nature, and any subsequent discovery or additional documents responsive to this request to produce should be supplied within thirty (30) days of first knowledge.

DEFINITIONS

A. "Document" or "documents" means any written, recorded, filmed, or graphic matter, whether produced, reproduced or on paper, cards, tapes, film, electronic facsimile, electronic or computer storage devices or any other media, including but not limited to, affidavits, agreements, applications, appointment calendars, emails, bills, bookkeeping entries, books, charts, checks, check stubs, communications, computer disks, correspondence, diaries, drawings, electronic mail, files, financial statements, graphs, handwritten notes, invoices, marginal notes or comments appearing in a document, memoranda, minutes, notebooks, notes, oral conversations, orders, pamphlets, periodicals, photographs, published materials of any kind, recordings, records, reports, sketches, statements, studies, summaries or records of meetings or conferences, summaries or records of personal conversations or interviews, summaries or records of telephone conversations, summaries or reports of investigations or negotiations, tax returns, telefaxes, telegrams, test results, or work papers, and also including but not limited to originals and all copies which are different in any way from the original whether by interlineation, receipt stamp, notation, indication of copies sent or received, or otherwise, drafts, and any and all other writings and data compilations which are in the possession, custody or control of Defendants or in the possession, custody, or control of the present or former agents, representatives or attorneys of Defendants, or any and all persons acting on Defendants' behalf, including documents at any time in the possession, custody or control of such individuals or entities or known by the Defendants to exist.

B. "Possession," "custody," and "control" mean a document in Defendants' physical custody, in the physical custody of Defendants' agents or attorneys, or, if it is in the physical custody of any other person, where Defendants: (a) owns such document in whole or in part; (b) has a right by contract, statute or otherwise to use, inspect, examine or copy such document on any terms; (c) has an understanding, express or implied, that Defendants may use, inspect, examine or copy such document on any terms; or (d) as a practical matter, been able to use, inspect, examine or copy such document when Defendants sought to do so.

C. "You", "your," "yours," or "Defendants" refers to Defendants, CFC, Ashley Alden, Chris Smart, Jess Henley, and Sami Myers, and any of Defendants' representatives, attorneys, agents or investigators.

D. "Plaintiff" means Logan Walter.

E. Where the singular is used with reference to any person, document or item, it will include the plural.

F. "Complaint" refers to the "Complaint and Demand for Jury Trial" filed in the Action.

G. Unless otherwise indicated, all words and terms used in this request shall have the same meaning as in the "Complaint."

DOCUMENTS TO BE PRODUCED

1. All documents and tangible things which in any way refer or relate to Plaintiff's terms and conditions of employment with CFC, including but not limited to any handbooks or written policies.

2. All documents and tangible things which in any way refer or relate to Plaintiff's duties and responsibilities with CFC.

3. All documents and tangible things which in any way refer or relate to Plaintiff's job performance at CFC.

4. All documents and tangible things which in any way refer or relate to any counseling or discipline of Plaintiff by CFC.

5. All documents and tangible things which in any way refer or relate to any internal grievances or complaints submitted by Plaintiff to CFC, including all documents related to the CFC corporate compliance division investigation of AOA in YEAR-1.

6. All documents and tangible things which in any way refer or relate to any complaints or incidents of alleged unlawful discrimination and/or retaliation against Plaintiff by CFC.

7. All documents related to the termination of Logan Walter.

8. Any calendars, diaries, or other documents that refer, that relate to, or contain any entries or notations pertaining to Plaintiff or AOA.

9. All documents and tangible things that refer, relate to, pertain to or contain any reference to or record of any communication between you and any current or former employee of CFC, concerning any issue raised in the pleadings in this Action or the allegations asserted by Plaintiff in the Complaint.

10. All documents and tangible things that refer, relate to, pertain to or contain any reference to or record of any damages, injuries, or losses suffered by Plaintiff as a result of Defendants' conduct as alleged in this Action.

11. All documents and tangible things that you relied upon when preparing your "Answer" to Plaintiff's Complaint, including affidavits, notes, and drafts of any and all documents.

12. All documents and tangible things that refer to, relate to, or are available to you supporting your contention that Defendants did not retaliate against Plaintiff.

13. Organizational charts for Citrus Florida Community Company January 1, YEAR-7 to the present.

14. A copy of CFC's corporate bylaws and articles of incorporation.

15. Any and all documents referencing or related to the AOA additive.

16. All documents, materials, and files located at the CFC Research Facility in Gulfport, Florida regarding or related to the AOA additive, including a copy of the original final AOA test results.

17. A copy of all sales contracts involving orange juice from January 1, YEAR-4 to the present.

18. Any and all sales records or data regarding the sale of orange juice from January 1, YEAR-4 to the present.

19. Documents evidencing Citrus Florida Community Company's total revenue and profitability from January 1, YEAR-4 to the present.

20. Documents evidencing Citrus Florida Community Company's total revenue from orange juice sales and profitability from January 1, YEAR-4 to the present.

21. Documents evidencing Citrus Florida Community Company's total revenue from orange juice with the AOA additive sales and profitability from January 1, YEAR-4 to the present.

22. Documents evidencing Citrus Florida Community Company encouraged and/or offered incentives to customers to purchase addition products, including orange juice, cleaning supplies, and air fresheners, at the end of each quarter to increase sales figures.

23. Copies of all Securities and Exchange Commission filing from January 1, YEAR-4 to the present.

24. Copies of all communications to investors from January 1, YEAR-4 to the present.

25. All documents regarding any reduction in force at CFC from January 1, YEAR-7 to the present.

26. All documents regarding stock options granted to the following employees, including all documents and information regarding the exercising of those options.

Jody Murray
Kim Vanguard
Cory Campbell
Lynn Smith
Ashley Alden
Chris Smart
Jess Henley
Dr. Sami Myers
Logan Walter

27. The human resources files, employment contracts, performance reviews, reprimands, awards, bonuses and payroll records of the following employees:

Jody Murray
Kim Vanguard
Cory Campbell
Lynn Smith
Ashley Alden
Chris Smart
Jess Henley
Dr. Sami Myers
Logan Walter

28. Any documents or materials provided by Defendants to any governmental agency (whether local, state, or federal) in response to a request for documents or subpoena from January 1, YEAR-1 to the present.

29. All documents Defendants may use at trial in support of their claim that they did not retaliate against Plaintiff and all documents Defendants may use at trial to assert a defense, including affirmative defenses, in this matter.

CERTIFICATE OF SERVICE

I HEREBY CERTIFY that the original and a true and correct copy of the foregoing has been furnished via U.S. Mail to Defense Counsel for CFC, Ashley Alden, Chris Smart, Jess Henley, and Sami Myers, this 7th day of December, YEAR-1.

Respectfully Submitted

s/ Jan Smartz
Jan Smartz, Esq.
Florida Bar No. 12345
Smartz and Associates, P.A.
123 Apple Way
Tampa, Florida 33601

Attachment N

STATE OF FLORIDA
IN THE CIRCUIT COURT FOR THE THIRTEENTH JUDICIAL CIRCUIT
IN AND FOR HILLSBOROUGH COUNTY, FLORIDA

LOGAN WALTER	)
	)
Plaintiff,	)
	)
vs.	)
	)
CITRUS FLORIDA COMMUNITY COMPANY, a Florida Corporation, ASHLEY ALDEN, CHRIS SMART, JESS HENLEY, SAMI MYERS, and LYNN SMITH	)
	)
Defendants.	)

NOTICE OF TAKING DEPOSITION OF DEFENDANT

PLEASE TAKE NOTICE that Plaintiff, Logan Walter, by and through their undersigned counsel, will take the deposition of Defendant, CENTRAL FLORDIA COMPANY. The deposition will be conducted upon oral examination before Orlando & Company, or other officer authorized by law to take depositions, at the following time and location:

DATE:	**Friday, 13 January YEAR-0**
TIME:	**9:00 a.m.**
DEPONENT:	**Citrus Florida Community Company, Defendant**
LOCATION:	**Orlando & Company** **Tampa, Florida**

This deposition is taken for the purpose of discovery, for use as evidence, and for such other uses and purposes as are permitted under the Florida Rules of Civil Procedure and other

applicable law. This deposition shall continue from day to day until completed.

PLEASE GOVERN YOURSELF ACCORDINGLY.

Respectfully Submitted

s/ Jan Smart

Jan Smartz, Esq.
Florida Bar No. 12345
Smartz and Associates, P.A.
123 Apple Way
Tampa, Florida 33601

CERTIFICATE OF SERVICE

I HEREBY CERTIFY that on December 7, YEAR-1, I electronically filed the foregoing with the Clerk of the Court, which will send a notice of electronic filing to counsel of record.

s/ Jan Smartz

STATE OF FLORIDA
IN THE CIRCUIT COURT FOR THE THIRTEENTH JUDICIAL CIRCUIT
IN AND FOR HILLSBOROUGH COUNTY, FLORIDA

LOGAN WALTER	)
	)
Plaintiff,	)
	)
vs.	)
	)
CITRUS FLORIDA COMMUNITY COMPANY, a Florida Corporation, ASHLEY ALDEN, CHRIS SMART, JESS HENLEY, SAMI MYERS, and LYNN SMITH	)
	)
Defendants.	)

NOTICE OF TAKING DEPOSITION OF DEFENDANT

PLEASE TAKE NOTICE that Plaintiff, Logan Walter, by and through their undersigned counsel, will take the deposition of Defendant, ASHLEY ALDEN. The deposition will be conducted upon oral examination before Orlando & Company, or other officer authorized by law to take depositions, at the following time and location:

DATE:	**Friday, 13 January YEAR-0**
TIME:	**9:00 a.m.**
DEPONENT:	**Ashley Alden, Defendant**
LOCATION:	**Orlando & Company** **Tampa, Florida**

This deposition is taken for the purpose of discovery, for use as evidence, and for such other uses and purposes as are permitted under the Florida Rules of Civil Procedure and other

applicable law. This deposition shall continue from day to day until completed.

PLEASE GOVERN YOURSELF ACCORDINGLY.

Respectfully Submitted

s/ Jan Smartz
Jan Smartz, Esq.
Florida Bar No. 12345
Smartz and Associates, P.A.
123 Apple Way
Tampa, Florida 33601

CERTIFICATE OF SERVICE

I HEREBY CERTIFY that on December 7, YEAR-1, I electronically filed the foregoing with the Clerk of the Court, which will send a notice of electronic filing to counsel of record.

s/ Jan Smartz

Attachment O

STATE OF FLORIDA
IN THE CIRCUIT COURT FOR THE THIRTEENTH JUDICIAL CIRCUIT
IN AND FOR HILLSBOROUGH COUNTY, FLORIDA

LOGAN WALTER	)
	)
Plaintiff,	)
	)
vs.	)
	)
CITRUS FLORIDA COMMUNITY COMPANY, a Florida Corporation, ASHLEY ALDEN, CHRIS SMART, JESS HENLEY, SAMI MYERS, and LYNN SMITH	)
	)
Defendants.	)

NOTICE OF TAKING DEPOSITION OF DEFENDANT

PLEASE TAKE NOTICE that Plaintiff, Logan Walter, by and through their undersigned counsel, will take the deposition of Defendant, CHRIS SMART. The deposition will be conducted upon oral examination before Orlando & Company, or other officer authorized by law to take depositions, at the following time and location:

DATE:	**Friday, 13 January YEAR-0**
TIME:	**9:00 a.m.**
DEPONENT:	**Chris Smart, Defendant**
LOCATION:	**Orlando & Company** **Tampa, Florida**

This deposition is taken for the purpose of discovery, for use as evidence, and for such other uses and purposes as are permitted under the Florida Rules of Civil Procedure and other

applicable law. This deposition shall continue from day to day until completed.

PLEASE GOVERN YOURSELF ACCORDINGLY.

Respectfully Submitted

s/ Jan Smartz
Jan Smartz, Esq.
Florida Bar No. 12345
Smartz and Associates, P.A.
123 Apple Way
Tampa, Florida 33601

CERTIFICATE OF SERVICE

I HEREBY CERTIFY that on December 7, YEAR-1, I electronically filed the foregoing with the Clerk of the Court, which will send a notice of electronic filing to counsel of record.

s/ Jan Smartz

STATE OF FLORIDA
IN THE CIRCUIT COURT FOR THE THIRTEENTH JUDICIAL CIRCUIT
IN AND FOR HILLSBOROUGH COUNTY, FLORIDA

LOGAN WALTER	)
	)
Plaintiff,	)
	)
vs.	)
	)
CITRUS FLORIDA COMMUNITY COMPANY, a Florida Corporation, ASHLEY ALDEN, CHRIS SMART, JESS HENLEY, SAMI MYERS, and LYNN SMITH	)
	)
Defendants.	)
______________________________________	)

NOTICE OF TAKING DEPOSITION OF DEFENDANT

PLEASE TAKE NOTICE that Plaintiff, Logan Walter, by and through their undersigned counsel, will take the deposition of Defendant, JESS HENLEY. The deposition will be conducted upon oral examination before Orlando & Company, or other officer authorized by law to take depositions, at the following time and location:

DATE:	**Friday, 13 January YEAR-0**
TIME:	**9:00 a.m.**
DEPONENT:	**Jess Henley, Defendant**
LOCATION:	**Orlando & Company** **Tampa, Florida**

This deposition is taken for the purpose of discovery, for use as evidence, and for such other uses and purposes as are permitted under the Florida Rules of Civil Procedure and other

applicable law. This deposition shall continue from day to day until completed.

PLEASE GOVERN YOURSELF ACCORDINGLY.

Respectfully Submitted

s/ Jan Smartz
Jan Smartz, Esq.
Florida Bar No. 12345
Smartz and Associates, P.A.
123 Apple Way
Tampa, Florida 33601

CERTIFICATE OF SERVICE

I HEREBY CERTIFY that on December 7, YEAR-1, I electronically filed the foregoing with the Clerk of the Court, which will send a notice of electronic filing to counsel of record.

s/ Jan Smartz

Attachment O

STATE OF FLORIDA
IN THE CIRCUIT COURT FOR THE THIRTEENTH JUDICIAL CIRCUIT
IN AND FOR HILLSBOROUGH COUNTY, FLORIDA

LOGAN WALTER	)
	)
Plaintiff,	)
	)
vs.	)
	)
CITRUS FLORIDA COMMUNITY COMPANY, a Florida Corporation, ASHLEY ALDEN, CHRIS SMART, JESS HENLEY, SAMI MYERS, and LYNN SMITH	)
	)
Defendants.	)
	)

NOTICE OF TAKING DEPOSITION OF DEFENDANT

PLEASE TAKE NOTICE that Plaintiff, Logan Walter, by and through their undersigned counsel, will take the deposition of Defendant, SAMI MYERS. The deposition will be conducted upon oral examination before Orlando & Company, or other officer authorized by law to take depositions, at the following time and location:

DATE:	**Friday, 13 January YEAR-0**
TIME:	**9:00 a.m.**
DEPONENT:	**Sami Myers, Defendant**
LOCATION:	**Orlando & Company** **Tampa, Florida**

This deposition is taken for the purpose of discovery, for use as evidence, and for such other uses and purposes as are permitted under the Florida Rules of Civil Procedure and other

applicable law. This deposition shall continue from day to day until completed.

PLEASE GOVERN YOURSELF ACCORDINGLY.

Respectfully Submitted

s/ Jan Smartz

Jan Smartz, Esq.
Florida Bar No. 12345
Smartz and Associates, P.A.
123 Apple Way
Tampa, Florida 33601

CERTIFICATE OF SERVICE

I HEREBY CERTIFY that on December 7, YEAR-1, I electronically filed the foregoing with the Clerk of the Court, which will send a notice of electronic filing to counsel of record.

s/ Jan Smartz

STATE OF FLORIDA
IN THE CIRCUIT COURT FOR THE THIRTEENTH JUDICIAL CIRCUIT
IN AND FOR HILLSBOROUGH COUNTY, FLORIDA

LOGAN WALTER	)
	)
Plaintiff,	)
	)
vs.	)
	)
CITRUS FLORIDA COMMUNITY COMPANY, a Florida Corporation, ASHLEY ALDEN, CHRIS SMART, JESS HENLEY, SAMI MYERS, and LYNN SMITH	)
	)
Defendants.	)

NOTICE OF TAKING DEPOSITION OF DEFENDANT

PLEASE TAKE NOTICE that Plaintiff, Logan Walter, by and through their undersigned counsel, will take the deposition of Defendant, LYNN SMITH. The deposition will be conducted upon oral examination before Orlando & Company, or other officer authorized by law to take depositions, at the following time and location:

DATE:	**Friday, 13 January YEAR-0**
TIME:	**9:00 a.m.**
DEPONENT:	**Lynn Smith, Defendant**
LOCATION:	**Orlando & Company** **Tampa, Florida**

This deposition is taken for the purpose of discovery, for use as evidence, and for such other uses and purposes as are permitted under the Florida Rules of Civil Procedure and other

applicable law. This deposition shall continue from day to day until completed.

PLEASE GOVERN YOURSELF ACCORDINGLY.

Respectfully Submitted

s/ Jan Smartz
Jan Smartz, Esq.
Florida Bar No. 12345
Smartz and Associates, P.A.
123 Apple Way
Tampa, Florida 33601

CERTIFICATE OF SERVICE

I HEREBY CERTIFY that on December 7, YEAR-1, I electronically filed the foregoing with the Clerk of the Court, which will send a notice of electronic filing to counsel of record.

s/ Jan Smartz

United States Securities and Exchange Commission
100 F Street, NE
Washington, DC 20549
Washington, D.C.

December 7, YEAR-1

Jody Murray
Chief Executive Officer
Citrus Florida Community Company
1941 Lay Road
Tampa, FL 33601

Re: Informal Investigation – Citrus Florida Community Company

Dear Murray:

The United States Securities and Exchange Commission has opened an informal inquiry into the events surrounding the launch of the AOA orange juice additive in YEAR-2. To assist the Securities and Exchange Commission with its investigation into this matter, we request that you voluntarily provide the documents requested in the attached document by 5:00pm on December 15, YEAR-1.

Should you have any questions regarding these requests, please do not hesitate to contact me at the below number.

Sincerely,

S. Heart

S. Heart
Securities and Exchange Commission
Headquarters
(111) 111-1111

Attachment P

INSTRUCTIONS AND DEFINITIONS

1. "Document" is used herein in the broadest sense of the term and means each and every writing or graphic matter of whatever nature, whether an original, a draft, or a copy, including all non-identical copies, however produced or reproduced, whether or not sent or received, and each and every tangible thing from which information can be processed or transcribed, such as tape or other electronic data communications. The term includes but is not limited to letters, records, forms, books, invoices, e-mail messages, e-mail attachments, electronically stored information, voicemail messages, checks, bills, receipts, diaries, calendars, logs, journals, notebooks, plans, directives, instructions, analyses, telegrams, studies, contracts, agreements, correspondence, communications, press releases, statistics, memoranda, notes, minutes, opinions, reports, summaries, worksheets, graphs, and charts and any other means by which information is recorded or transmitted, including but not limited to audio, visual, and digital recordings, photographs (positive prints and negatives), slides, films, phonorecords, teletypes, telefax, facsimiles, thermafax, microfilm, punch cards, computer data, cloud data, printouts and data processing records, translated, if necessary, by the respondent through detection devices into reasonably usable form.

2. The terms "and" and "or" should be construed conjunctively or disjunctively, whichever makes the request more inclusive.

3. The terms "any" and "all" should be construed as "any and all."

4. The use of the singular form of any word includes the plural and vice versa.

5. For purposes of this request, the time period applicable to the following requests is January 1, YEAR-4, to the present ("the applicable time period") unless otherwise noted.

6. The response to this request shall be continuing in nature so as to require a supplemental response in the event that, after responding to any individual request, you obtain or become aware of additional information responsive to any request.

DOCUMENTS REQUESTED

1. Any and all documents related to the scientific testing of the AOA additive, including, but not limited to, raw test data and reports and/or memoranda discussing such test data.

2. All CFC Board meeting agendas discussing the AOA additive and all CFC Board meeting minutes in which the AOA additive is discussed.

Attachment P

3. With regard to the following individuals: Jody Murray, Kim Vanguard, Tracy Strain, Cory Campbell, Lynn Smith, Ashley Alden, Chris Smart, Jess Henely, Logan Walter, Jamie Tate, Sami Myers:

    a. All communications, including, but not limited to, email and letter communications, between the above individuals that include reference to the AOA additive.

    b. All communications, including, but not limited to, email and letter communications, between the above individuals regarding the sale or marketing of orange juice from September 1, YEAR-2 to February 1, YEAR-1.

    c. All corporate calendars and diaries of the above individuals.

    d. The human resources employment files on the above individuals.

    e. The payment records of the above individuals, including bonus payments.

    f. Copies of any and all internal investigation materials containing mention of any of the above individuals, including, but not limited to, corporate compliance office files.

4. Copies of any and all internal investigation materials related to AOA, including, but not limited to corporate compliance office files.

5. A list of all stock option grants to Jody Murray, Kim Vanguard, Tracy Strain, Cory Campbell, Lynn Smith, Ashley Alden, Chris Smart, Jess Henely, Logan Walter, Jamie Tate, Sami Myers.

6. A list of when all stock options vested for Jody Murray, Kim Vanguard, Tracy Strain, Cory Campbell, Lynn Smith, Ashley Alden, Chris Smart, Jess Henely, Logan Walter, Jamie Tate, Sami Myers.

7. A list of all stock options exercised by Jody Murray, Kim Vanguard, Tracy Strain, Cory Campbell, Lynn Smith, Ashley Alden, Chris Smart, Jess Henely, Logan Walter, Jamie Tate, Sami Myers.

8. All documents regarding any stock option grants to Jody Murray, Kim Vanguard, Tracy Strain, Cory Campbell, Lynn Smith, Ashley Alden, Chris Smart, Jess Henely, Logan Walter, Jamie Tate, Sami Myers.

9. A copy of all sales contracts involving orange juice from January 1, YEAR-2 to January 1, YEAR-0.

10. Any and all sales records or data regarding the sale of orange juice containing the AOA additive.

11. Any and all sales records or data regarding the sale of orange juice from September 1,

YEAR-2 through February 1, YEAR-1.

12. All purchase records for the sale of orange juice containing the AOA additive.

13. All purchase records for the sale of orange juice from January 1, YEAR-2 to January 1, YEAR-0.

14. Documents sufficient to show Citrus Florida Community Company's total revenue and Profitability (gross and net) from January 1, YEAR-7 to present.

15. Documents sufficient to show Citrus Florida Community Company's total revenue from orange juice sales and profitability (gross and net) from January 1, YEAR-7 to the present.

16. Documents sufficient to show Citrus Florida Community Company's total revenue from orange juice with the AOA additive sales and profitability (gross and net) from January 1, YEAR-7 to the present.

17. All contracts or sales agreements entered into or modified by CFC from January 1, YEAR-4 to the present for the sale of product. This request applies to all product lines distributed by CFC, including, but not limited to, orange juice, cleaning supplies, air fresheners, and other citrus based products.

18. All documents evidencing the amount of product sold by CFC from January 1, YEAR-4 to the present. This request applies to all product lines distributed by CFC, including, but not limited to, orange juice, cleaning supplies, air fresheners, and other citrus based products.

19. All documents evidencing the amount of product shipped to customer from January 1, YEAR-4 to the present and the shipping dates such product was shipped. This request applies to all product lines distributed by CFC, including, but not limited to, orange juice, cleaning supplies, air fresheners, and other citrus based products.

20. The names of all employees responsible for selling product lines for CFC.

21. Copies of all Securities and Exchange Commission filing from January 1, YEAR-4 to the present.

22. Copies of all quarterly revenue statements published or made available to investors, analysts, or the public from January 1, YEAR-4 to the present.

23. All documents provided or made available to investors from January 1, YEAR-2 to the present.

24. Copies of all statements, whether written or verbal, made to investors from January 1, YEAR-2 to the present.

UNITED STATESSECURITIES AND EXCHANGE COMMISSION

Washington, D.C. 20549

Notice on Supplying Information Voluntarily

When we request that you provide information to us voluntarily, the Privacy Act of 1974 requires that we tell you how we can use the information and that we cannot sanction you if you fail to provide all or any part of it to us. However, as discussed below, sanctions may apply if you provide false or misleading information to us. Various laws authorize the Securities and Exchange Commission ("SEC") to request information from you: Sections 19 and 20 of the Securities Act of 1933, Section21 of the Securities Exchange Act of 1934, Section 321of the Trust Indenture Act of 1939, Section 42 of the In- vestment Company Act of 1940, Section 209 of the Investment Advisers Act of 1940 and Title 17 of the Code of Federal Regulations, Section 202.5.

How We May Use Your Information

Our principal purpose for requesting information from you is to respond to inquiries and complaints from the public. The SEC may also use your information to determine whether any person has violated, is violating, or is about to violate any provision of the federal securities laws or rules that the SEC enforces, such as the rules of the securities exchanges and the Municipal Securities Rulemaking Board. The SEC may use the information you provide in an enforcement proceeding. If the information you provide points to violations of other laws or regulations, we may turn your information over to other governmental agencies, including United States Attorneys and state prosecutors. We generally do not disclose to you whether we have done so or not. The SEC will not agree to limit its use of your information in any way, unless the SEC or its staff explicitly agrees to do so in writing.

Routine Uses of the Information You May Provide

Listed below are the ways we may routinely use your information: 1.To coordinate law enforcement activities between the SEC and other federal, state, local or foreign law enforcement agencies, securities self- regulatory organizations, and foreign securities authorities. 2. By SEC personnel for purposes of investigating possible violations of, or to conduct investigations authorized by the federal securities laws. 3. Where there is an indication of a violation or potential violation of law, whether civil, criminal or regulatory in nature, and whether arising by general statute or particular program statute, or by regulation, rule or order issued pursuant thereto, the relevant records in the system of records may be referred to the appropriate agency, whether federal, state, or local, a foreign governmental authority or foreign securities authority, or a securities self-regulatory organization charged with the responsibility of investigating or prosecuting such violation or charged with enforcing or implementing the statute or rule, regulation or order issued pursuant thereto. 4. In any proceeding where the federal securities laws are in issue or in which the Commission, or past or present members of its staff, is a party or otherwise involved in an official capacity. 5. To a federal, state, local or foreign governmental authority or foreign securities authority maintaining civil, criminal or other relevant enforcement information or other pertinent information, such as current licenses, if necessary to obtain information relevant to an agency decision concerning hiring or retention of an employee, the issuance of a security clearance, the letting of a contract, or the issuance of a license, grant or other benefit. 6. To a federal, state, local or foreign governmental authority or foreign securities authority, in response to its request, in connection with the hiring or retention of an employee, the issuance of a security clearance, the reporting of an investigation of an employee, the letting of a contract, or the issuance of a license, grant or other benefit by the requesting agency, to the extent that the information is relevant and necessary to the requesting agency's decision on the matter. 7. In connection with proceedings by the Commission pursuant to Rule 102(e) of its Rules of Practice 17 CFR201.102(e). 8. When considered appropriate, records in this system maybe disclosed to a bar association, the American Institute of Certified Public Accountants, a state accountancy board or other federal, state, local or foreign licensing or oversight authority, foreign securities authority, or professional association or self-regulatory authority performing similar functions, for possible disciplinary or other action. 9. In connection with investigations or disciplinary proceedings by a state securities regulatory authority, a foreign securities authority, or by a self-regulatory organization involving one or more of its members. 10. As a data source for management information for production of summary descriptive statistics and analytical studies in support of the function for which the records are collected and maintained or for statistical information (without personal identification of individuals) under the Freedom of Information Act or to locate specific individuals for personnel research or other personnel management functions.11. In connection with their regulatory and enforcement responsibilities mandated by the federal securities laws (as defined in Section 21(g) of the Securities Exchange Act of 1934, 15 U.S.C. 78u(g)), or state or foreign laws regulating securities or other related matters, records may be disclosed to national securities associations that are registered with the Commission, the Municipal Securities Rulemaking Board, the Securities Investor Protection

Corporation, the federal banking authorities, including but not limited to, the Board of Governors of the Federal Reserve System, the Comptroller of the Currency, and the Federal Deposit Insurance Corporation, state securities regulatory or law enforcement agencies or organizations, or regulatory law enforcement agencies of a foreign government, or foreign securities authority.12.To any trustee, receiver, master, special counsel, or other individual or entity that is appointed by a court of competent jurisdiction or as a result of an agreement between the parties in connection with litigation or administrative proceedings involving allegations of violations of the federal securities laws (as defined in Section 21(g) of the Securities Exchange Act of 1934, 15 U.S.C. 78u(g)) or the Commission's Rules of Practice, 17 CFR 202.1 et seq., or otherwise, where such trustee, receiver, master, special counsel or other individual or entity is specifically designated to perform particular functions with respect to, or as a result of, the pending action or proceeding or in connection with the administration and enforcement by the Com- mission of the federal securities laws or the Commission's Rules of Practice.13. To any persons during the course of any inquiry or investigation conducted by the Commission's staff, or in connection with civil litigation, if the staff has reason to believe that the person to whom the record is disclosed may have further information about the matters related therein, and those matters appeared to be relevant at the time to the subject matter of the inquiry.14.To any person with whom the Commission contracts to re-produce, by typing, photocopy or other means, any record within this system for use by the Commission and its staff in connection with their official duties or to any person who is utilized by the Commission to perform clerical or stenographic functions relating to the official business of the Commission. 15. Inclusion in reports published by the Commission pursuant to authority granted in the federal securities laws (as defined in Section 21(g) of the Securities Exchange Act of1934, 15 U.S.C. 78u(g)).16. To members of advisory committees that are created by the Commission or by the Congress to render advice and recommendations to the Commission or to the Congress, to be used solely in connection with their official designated functions.17. To any person who is or has agreed to be subject to the Commission's Rules of Conduct, 17 CFR 200.735-1 et seq., and who assists in the investigation by the Commission of possible violations of securities laws (as defined in Section 21 (g) of the Securities Exchange Act of 1934, 15U.S.C. 78u (g)), in the preparation or conduct of enforcement actions brought by the Commission for such violations, or otherwise in connection with the Commission's enforcement or regulatory functions under the federal securities laws.18. Disclosure may be made to a Congressional office from the record of an individual in response to an inquiry from the Congressional office made at the request of that individual.19.

To respond to inquiries from Members of Congress, the press and the public which relate to specific matters that the Commission has investigated and to matters under the Commission's jurisdiction. 20. To prepare and publish information relating to violations of the federal securities laws as provided in Section 21(a)of the Securities Exchange Act of 1934, 15 U.S.C. 78u(a), as amended. 21. To respond to subpoenas in any litigation or other proceeding. 22. To a trustee in bankruptcy.

False Statements and Documents
Section 1001 of Title 18 of the United States Code pro-vides as follows: Whoever, in any matter within the jurisdiction of any department or agency of the United States knowingly and willfully falsifies, conceals, or covers up by any trick, scheme, or de-vice a material fact, or makes any false, fictitious or fraudulent statements or representations, or makes or uses any false writing or document knowing the same to contain any false, fictitious or fraudulent statement or entry, shall be fined under this title or imprisoned not more than five years, or both.

The information you give the SEC may be used against you in any federal, state, local or foreign administrative, civil or criminal proceeding brought by the Commission or any other agency. You may refuse to give any information that may tend to incriminate you or subject you to fine, penalty or forfeiture in accordance with the rights guaranteed to you by the Fifth Amendment to the Constitution of the United States.

The Freedom of Information Act
The Freedom of Information Act (FOIA) generally allows the SEC to make your information available to the public upon request. You may request that your information not be released to the public by writing a letter asking that it remain confidential under one of the exemptions de-scribed in FOIA. See 5 United States Code, Section 552.The SEC determines whether your claim of an exemption is valid when someone requests your information under FOIA. Rule 83 of the SEC's Rules on Information and Requests (17 CFR, section 200.83) explains how you should make your request for confidentiality. Your letter may be sent or faxed to our FOIA Officer at 450 Fifth Street, N.W.,MS 0-5, Washington, DC 20549 or fax # (555) 555-5555.

U.S. Department of Justice

The United States Attorney's Office
Southern District of New York
1 St. Andrew's Plaza
New York City, NY 10007

Re: Request for Documents

December 7, YEAR-1

Jody Murray
Chief Executive Officer
Citrus Florida Community Company
1941 Lay Road
Tampa, FL 33601

Dear Murray:

The United States Attorney's Office for the Southern District of New York has opened an investigation into the use of the AOA additive by the Citrus Florida Community Company. To assist the United States Attorney's Office with its investigation into this matter, we request that you respond to the attached request for documents by 5:00pm on December 15, YEAR-1.

Should you have any questions regarding these requests, please do not hesitate to contact me at the below number.

Sincerely,

J. Smiley

J. Smiley
Asst. United States Attorney
(111) 111-1111

Attachment Q

INSTRUCTIONS AND DEFINITIONS

1. "Document" is used herein in the broadest sense of the term and means each and every writing or graphic matter of whatever nature, whether an original, a draft, or a copy, including all non-identical copies, however produced or reproduced, whether or not sent or received, and each and every tangible thing from which information can be processed or transcribed, such as tape or other electronic data communications. The term includes but is not limited to letters, records, forms, books, invoices, e-mail messages, e-mail attachments, electronically stored information, voicemail messages, checks, bills, receipts, diaries, calendars, logs, journals, notebooks, plans, directives, instructions, analyses, telegrams, studies, contracts, agreements, correspondence, communications, press releases, statistics, memoranda, notes, minutes, opinions, reports, summaries, worksheets, graphs, and charts and any other means by which information is recorded or transmitted, including but not limited to audio, visual, and digital recordings, photographs (positive prints and negatives), slides, films, phonorecords, teletypes, telefax, facsimiles, thermafax, microfilm, punch cards, computer data, cloud data, printouts and data processing records, translated, if necessary, by the respondent through detection devices into reasonably usable form.

2. The terms "and" and "or" should be construed conjunctively or disjunctively, whichever makes the request more inclusive.

3. The terms "any" and "all" should be construed as "any and all."

4. The use of the singular form of any word includes the plural and vice versa.

5. For purposes of this subpoena duces tecum, the time period applicable to the following requests is January 1, YEAR-4, to the present ("the applicable time period") unless otherwise noted.

6. The response to this request shall be continuing in nature so as to require a supplemental response in the event that, after responding to any individual request, you obtain or become aware of additional information responsive to any request.

DOCUMENTS REQUESTED

1. Any and all documents related to the scientific testing of the AOA additive, including, but not limited to, raw test data and reports and/or memoranda discussing such test data.

2. All CFC Board meeting agendas discussing the AOA additive and all CFC Board meeting minutes in which the AOA additive is discussed.

3. With regard to the following individuals: Jody Murray, Kim Vanguard, Tracy Strain, Cory Campbell, Lynn Smith, Ashley Alden, Chris Smart, Jess Henley, Logan Walter, Jamie Tate, Sami Myers

    a. All communications, including, but not limited to, email and letter communications, between the above individuals that include reference to the AOA additive.

    b. All communications, including, but not limited to, email and letter communications, between the above individuals regarding the sale or marketing of orange juice from September 1, YEAR-2 to February 1, YEAR-1.

    c. All corporate calendars and diaries of the above individuals.

    d. The human resources employment files on the above individuals.

    e. The payment records of the above individuals, including bonus payments.

    f. Copies of any and all internal investigation materials containing mention of any of the above individuals, including, but not limited to, corporate compliance office files.

    g. All documents evidencing the granting or excising of stock option by the above individuals.

4. Copies of any and all internal investigation materials related to AOA, including, but not limited to, corporate compliance office files.

Attachment Q

STATE OF NEW YORK
OFFICE OF THE ATTORNEY GENERAL

JAKE YORK
ATTORNEY GENERAL

DIVISION OF ECONOMIC JUSTICE
CONSUMER FRAUDS BUREAU

December 10,
YEAR-1

BY EMAIL
AND FIRST CLASS MAIL

Jody Murray
Chief Executive Officer
Citrus Florida Community Company
1941 Lay Road
Tampa, FL 33601

Re: Acceptance of Subpoena Duces Tecum

Dear Murray:

As registered agent of Citrus Florida Community Company, please sign below to confirm that you accept service of the enclosed Subpoena Duces Tecum served on the Citrus Florida Community Company. In addition, we request that Citrus Florida Community Company comply fully with the Subpoena Duces Tecum by Monday, February 13, YEAR-0 by 5:00 pm.

Please sign below and fax a return copy to me at (212) 222-2222 and mail the original for our records. If you have any questions, please contact me at (212) 111-1111. Thank you.

Sincerely,

Susan New

Susan New
Assistant Attorney General
Consumer Frauds Bureau

Enclosures

Acceptance of Subpoena Duces Tecum, dated December __, YEAR-1,
by: Citrus Florida Community Company

____

By: Jody Murray

Attachment R

OFFICE OF THE ATTORNEY GENERAL
OF THE STATE OF NEW YORK

In the Matter of the Investigation by JAKE YORK, Attorney General of the State of New York, relating to Orange Juice Additive.	**SUBPOENA DUCES TECUM**

THE PEOPLE OF THE STATE OF NEW YORK

To: Citrus Florida Community Company
1941 Lay Road
Tampa, FL 33624

PLEASE TAKE NOTICE THAT YOU ARE HEREBY REQUIRED, pursuant to the laws of the State of New York, including New York Executive Law § 63(12), to deliver and turn over to Attorney General, Jake York, Attention Susan New, Assistant Attorney General, 120 Broadway, Twenty-Sixth Floor, New York, New York, 10271-0332, all documents that are in your possession, custody, or control requested in the attached Schedule entitled "Documents to be Produced" by 5:00 pm on Monday, February 13, YEAR-0, in accordance with the instructions, rules of construction and definitions to use to respond to this subpoena set forth below in the Schedule entitled "Instructions and Definitions."

PLEASE TAKE NOTICE that the Attorney General deems seeking the information to be in the public interest, and deems the information sought relevant and material to a confidential investigation concerning possible violations of New York General Business Law § 349, New York General Business Law § 350, Executive Law § 63(12), and related statutes.

Attachment R

PLEASE TAKE NOTICE that your failure to comply fully with this subpoena on the date, time and place stated above, or at an agreed upon adjourned date and time, may subject you to prosecution for a misdemeanor or civil contempt proceedings pursuant to the laws of the State of New York, including New York Civil Practice Law and Rules § 2308. You may be liable, in addition to any other lawful punishment, for the damages sustained by the State of New York, and for a penalty not to exceed fifty dollars ($50.00).

PLEASE TAKE NOTICE that the Attorney General designates, for purposes of jurisdiction and venue, in any action or proceeding (a "Case") arising out of this subpoena or the investigation in which this subpoena is issued, including any Case alleging a violation of law or seeking to enforce this subpoena: (a) the Supreme Court of the State of New York, County of New York; or (b) alternatively, any other Court of competent jurisdiction.

WITNESS JAKE YORK, Attorney General of the State of New York, this 10th day of December, YEAR-1.

JAKE YORK
Attorney General of the
State of New York

By: *Susan New*

Susan New
Assistant Attorney General
Consumer Frauds Bureau
120 Broadway, Suite 26C
New York, New York 10271

PLEASE DIRECT ALL INQUIRIES CONCERNING THIS SUBPOENA TO ASSISTANT ATTORNEY GENERAL SUSAN NEW AT (212) 111-1111.

INSTRUCTIONS AND DEFINITIONS

1. "Citrus Florida Community Company" means Citrus Florida Community Company and (i) its directors, officers, agents, employees, attorneys, or any other person acting on its behalf and (ii) any predecessor, successor, parent corporation, subsidiary, division, or affiliate, wherever located.

2. "Orange Juice Additive" means any additive to the orange juice brands produced by Citrus Florida Community Company, specifically the AOA additive.

3. "AOA additive" means the additive created and/ or produced by Central Florida Company and added in Citrus Florida Community Company's orange juice brands beginning in October 26, YEAR-2, until the discontinuation of the product on or around January 1, YEAR-1.

4. "Agreement" shall include any contract, memorandum of intent, letter of intent, terms sheet, framework agreement, outline agreement, and any amendment or modification, predecessor or superseding agreement, and any other agreement or understanding referenced in or ancillary to the agreement.

5. "Document" is used herein in the broadest sense of the term and means each and every writing or graphic matter of whatever nature, whether an original, a draft, or a copy, including all non-identical copies, however produced or reproduced, whether or not sent or received, and each and every tangible thing from which information can be processed or transcribed, such as tape or other electronic data communications. The term includes but is not limited to electronically stored information, letters, records, forms, books, invoices, e-mail messages, e-mail attachments, voicemail messages, checks, bills, receipts, diaries, calendars, logs, journals, notebooks, plans, directives, instructions, analyses, telegrams, studies, contracts, agreements, correspondence, communications, press releases, statistics, memoranda, notes, minutes, opinions, reports, summaries, worksheets, graphs, and charts and any other means by which information is recorded or transmitted, including but not limited to audio, visual, and digital recordings, photographs (positive prints and negatives), slides, films, phonorecords, teletypes, telefax, facsimiles, thermafax, microfilm, punch cards, computer data, cloud data, printouts and data processing records, translated, if necessary, by the respondent through detection devices into reasonably usable form.

6. “Electronic hard drive” shall include the primary storage unit of a desktop computer, laptop computer and / or other computer devices, consisting of one or more magnetic media platters on which digital data can be written or erased magnetically.

7. “Electronic hard disk” shall include any peripheral data storage device that may be found inside, or attached to, a desktop computer, laptop computer, and other computer devices.

8. “Concerning” means referring to, related to, describing, reflecting, regarding, evidencing, recording, memorializing, comprising, constituting, or supporting, directly or indirectly.

9. The terms “and” and “or” should be construed conjunctively or disjunctively, whichever makes the request more inclusive.

10. The terms “any” and “all” should be construed as “any and all.”

11. The use of the singular form of any word includes the plural and vice versa.

12. For purposes of this subpoena duces tecum, the time period applicable to the following requests is August 1, YEAR-2, to the present (“the applicable time period”) unless otherwise noted. A request for a schedule, agreement, or other document for the applicable time period encompasses any schedule, agreement, or other document created, in use, or in effect during any part of the applicable time period. Production is also required if a specific request pre-dates the applicable time period.

13. Each document submitted in compliance herewith should be numbered consecutively on the face of the document and should clearly identify the paragraph of the subpoena to which the document is responsive, unless original documents are being produced for inspection and copying. All copies of original documents should be legible in their entirety and produced electronically, preferably in a single page .tif format that is readable by Concordance with Opticon. The load file should include the following categories: begin doc, end doc, page count and the corresponding Optical Character Recognition (“OCR”) text file.

14. If any document the production of which is called for by this subpoena duces tecum is withheld on the ground of purported privilege, for each such document please provide the following information in writing on the return date of this subpoena:

(i) the purported legal ground for withholding the document;

(ii) the type of document;

(iii) the general subject matter of the document;

(iv) the date of the document;

(v) the author of the document;

(vi) all recipients of the document; and

(vii) such other information as is sufficient to identify the document for a motion to a court to compel its production.

15. If any of the documents called for in this subpoena have been produced to any individual, organization, corporation, governmental agency, or any other entity, please provide the Attorney General with a description of such documents and the individual(s) or entity(s) to which such documents have been produced.

16. If any of the documents called for in this subpoena have previously been produced to the Attorney General, please identify by Bates number (i) each such document and (ii) the subpoena call to which the document is responsive.

17. The response to this subpoena duces tecum shall be continuing in nature so as to require a supplemental response in the event that, after responding to any individual request, you obtain or become aware of additional information responsive to any request.

DOCUMENTS TO BE PRODUCED

1. All e-mails and e-mail attachments sent or received between August 1, YEAR-2 to present by all employees of Citrus Florida Community Company who had any involvement with or responsibility concerning the AOA additive.

2. All e-mails and e-mail attachments sent or received between August 1, YEAR-2 to present by the following individuals:

Jody Murray
Kim Vanguard
Cory Campbell
Lynn Smith
Ashley Alden
Chris Smart
Jess Henley
Dr. Sami Myers
Logan Walter

3. All telephone, including mobile telephone, records, including, but not limited to, all telephone billing records sufficient to show telephone calls made or received by (a) all employees of Citrus Florida Community Company who had any involvement with or responsibility concerning the AOA additive and (b) each individual listed in Paragraph 1(b) above (to the extent not included in section (a) of this paragraph).

4. All electronic and / or hardcopy calendars, appointment books, diaries, and / or similar documents utilized and maintained by (a) all employees of Citrus Florida Community Company who had any involvement with or responsibility concerning the AOA additive and (b) each individual listed in Paragraph 1(b) above (to the extent not included in section (a) of this paragraph).

5. All electronic hard drives, electronic hard disks, and network drives utilized by Ashley Alden, Chris Smart, Jess Henley, Dr. Sami Myers, and Logan Walter.

6. All documents regarding the AOA additive, including, but not limited to, all documents regarding scientific research, marketing research, product pricing, product placement, product profitability estimates, contracts, agreements, and correspondence.

7. All documents regarding or related to the Citrus Florida Community Company's internal investigation of alleged misconduct regarding the use of the AOA additive, including, but not limited to, all documents related to the internal investigation related to the allegations of

Attachment R

Logan Walter.

8. All documents concerning any communications, agreements, or arrangements between Citrus Florida Community Company and any entity that purchased or sold the orange juice produced by Citrus Florida Community Company between August 1, YEAR-2 and the present.

9. All documents concerning any communications, agreements, or arrangements between Citrus Florida Community Company and any entity that purchased or sold the AOA orange juice produced by Citrus Florida Community Company between August 1, YEAR-2 and the present.

10. Documents sufficient to show Citrus Florida Community Company's total revenue and profitability (gross and net) for the applicable time period.

11. Documents sufficient to show Citrus Florida Community Company's total revenue from orange juice sales and profitability (gross and net) for the applicable time period.

12. Documents sufficient to show Citrus Florida Community Company's total revenue from orange juice with the AOA additive sales and profitability (gross and net) for the applicable time period.

13. Organizational charts for Citrus Florida Community Company for the applicable time period.

Campbell, Cory

From: Murray, Jody
Sent: Saturday, March 26, YEAR-1
06:20 AM
To: Campbell, Cory
Subject: RE: AOA Issue

Thanks, Corey. I really appreciate your handling this situation. It's nice to know that you are my attorney.

From: Campbell, Cory
Sent: Friday, March 25, YEAR-1
05:32PM
To: Murray, Jody
Subject: AOA Issues

Smith completed internal investigation. Problems arose, but they're history now. No need to worry about a leak. We represent the company. These conversations are privileged, but the privilege belongs to the company and the company decides whether to waive it. If there is a conflict, the attorney-client privilege belongs to the company.

Cory Campbell

CERTIFICATE OF APPRECIATION

AWARDED TO

ASHLEY ALDEN

For Outstanding Company Work

We couldn't do it without you!

Awarded this 15th day of April, YEAR-1

Jody Murray
Citrus Florida Community Company, CEO

Attachment T

CERTIFICATE OF APPRECIATION

AWARDED TO

CHRIS SMART

For Outstanding Company Work

We couldn't do it without you!

Awarded this 15th day of April, YEAR-1

Jody Murray

CENTRAL FLORIDA CAWARDED TO

Attachment T

CERTIFICATE OF APPRECIATION

AWARDED TO

JESS HENLEY

For Outstanding Company Work

We couldn't do it without you!

Awarded this 15th day of April, YEAR-1

Jody Murray
Citrus Florida Community Company, CEO

Attachment T

Deferred Prosecution Agreement

The Defendant, Citrus Florida Community Company (hereinafter "CFC"), by its undersigned attorney, pursuant to the authority granted by its Board of Directors, and the United States Attorney's Office for the Middle District of Florida (the "Office") enter into this Deferred Prosecution Agreement (hereinafter "the Agreement"). Except as specifically provided below, the Agreement shall be in effect for a period of two (2) years from the date it is fully executed.

The Criminal Information

1. CFC shall waive indictment and agree to the filing of a one count Information (hereinafter "the Information") in the United States District Court for the Middle District of Florida charging it with wire fraud in violation of 18 U.S.C. § 1343.

Acceptance of Responsibility

2. CFC accepts and acknowledges responsibility for its behavior as set forth in the Statement of Facts attached hereto and incorporated by reference herein as Appendix A (hereinafter "Statement of Facts"), which led to the charges in paragraph 1.

Agreement

3. In light of CFC's remedial actions to date and its willingness to (a) undertake additional remediation; (b) acknowledge responsibility for its behavior; (c) continue its cooperation with the Office and other governmental regulatory agencies; (d) demonstrate its future good conduct and full compliance with all laws and regulations; (e) agree to pay a fine pursuant to paragraph 4 below; and (f) agree to the appointment of an independent monitor selected by CFC and approved by the Office; the Office shall recommend to the Court that prosecution of CFC on the criminal Information filed pursuant to paragraph 1 be deferred for a period of twenty-four (24) months from the filing date of the criminal complaint. If CFC fully complies with all the obligations under this Agreement, within thirty (30) days of this Agreement's expiration, the Office will seek dismissal with prejudice of the criminal information filed against CFC as described in paragraph 1. If the Court declines to defer prosecution for any reason, this Agreement shall be null and void, and the parties will revert to their pre-Agreement positions.

Fine and Restitution

4. CFC agrees that it will pay a total of Twenty-Five Million ($25,000,000.00) Dollars to the United States as part of this Agreement, which payments are attributable to the following: a fine consisting of Twenty Million (20,000,000.00) Dollars and a compensation fund for victims of Five Million ($5,000,000.00) Dollars. The monetary criminal penalty shall be paid in four equal installments paid yearly starting on May 31 YEAR-0, and each May 31st thereafter. The funds

payable for the compensation fund will be paid within ten (10) days following the court's acceptance of this Agreement.

Appointment of an Independent Monitor

5. CFC agrees to the appointment of an independent monitor selected by CFC and approved by the Office. It shall be a condition of the Monitor's retention that the Monitor is independent of CFC and that no attorney-client relationship shall be formed between the Monitor and CFC. The Monitor shall:

a. Monitor CFC's compliance with this Agreement, and have authority to require CFC to take any steps they believe are necessary to comply with the terms of this Agreement;

b. Report to the Office, on at least a quarterly basis and between thirty (30) and forty-five (45) calendar days after the court approval of this Agreement, as to CFC's compliance with this Agreement and the implementation and effectiveness of the internal controls, financial reporting, disclosure processes and related compliance functions of the Company.

6. CFC agrees that if the Monitor resigns or is unable to serve the balance of their term, a successor shall be selected by CFC and approved by the Office within forty-five (45) days. CFC agrees that all provisions in this Agreement that apply to the Monitor shall apply to any successor Monitor.

7. CFC agrees that the Chief Executive Officer and General Counsel of CFC will meet quarterly with the Office and the Monitor, in conjunction with the Monitor's quarterly reports.

8. CFC shall adopt all recommendations contained in each report submitted by the Monitor to the Office unless CFC objects to the recommendation and the Office agrees that adoption of the recommendation should not be required.

9. CFC agrees that the Monitor may also disclose their reports, as directed by the Office, to any other federal or state law enforcement or regulatory agency in furtherance of an investigation of any other matters discovered by, or brought to the attention of, the Office in connection with the Office's investigation of CFC or the implementation of this Agreement.

Training and Education

10. CFC agrees that it will establish and maintain a training and education program, which shall be reviewed and approved by the Independent Monitor, designed to advance and underscore CFC's commitment to exemplary corporate citizenship, to best practices of effective corporate governance and the highest principles of integrity and professionalism, and to fostering a culture of openness, accountability and compliance throughout CFC.

11. CFC shall endow a chair at Stetson University College of Law dedicated to the teaching of business ethics and corporate governance, which position shall include conducting one of more seminars per year on business ethics and corporate governance at Stetson University College of Law that members of CFC's executive and management staff, along with representatives of executive and management staffs of other companies in the Tampa area, may attend.

Cooperation

12. CFC acknowledges and understands that its cooperation with the criminal investigation by the Office is an important and material factor underlying the Office's decision to enter into this Agreement, and, therefore CFC agrees to cooperate fully and actively with the Office and any other federal agency regarding any matter relating to the Office's investigation about which CFC has knowledge or information. CFC agrees that its continuing cooperation with the Office's investigation shall include, but not be limited to, the following:

a. CFC agrees to completely and truthfully disclose all information in its possession as requested by the Office, including but not limited to all information about activities of CFC, present and former employees, directors, officers, and agents of CFC.

b. CFC agrees that it shall provide to the Office, on request, any relevant document, electronic data, or other object in CFC's possession, custody and/or control concerning any matter charged in the Information subject to the applicable laws and regulations. Whenever such data is in electronic format, CFC shall provide access to such data and assistance in operating computer and other equipment as necessary to retrieve the data. If such documents, data or other objects are in overseas locations, CFC will make reasonable efforts to make the items available within the United States.

c. CFC agrees that its obligations to cooperate will continue even after the deferred prosecution period as defined in paragraph 3, so long as any individual or entity is subject to prosecution, or while any related appeal is pending.

d. With respect to any information, testimony, documents, records or physical evidence provided by CFC to the Office or a grand jury, CFC consents to any and all disclosures of such materials to such designated agencies as the Office, in its sole discretion, deems appropriate. With respect to any such materials that constitute "matters occurring before the grand jury" within the meaning of Federal Rule of Criminal Procedure 6(e), CFC further consents to: (I) any order sought by the Office permitting such disclosures; and (II) Office's *ex parte* or *in camera* application for such orders.

13. The obligation to cooperate is not intended to apply in the event that a prosecution against CFC is pursued and not deferred.

Public Statements by CFC

14. CFC expressly agrees that it shall not, through its attorneys, board of directors, agents, officers, employees, or any other representative make or adopt any public statement contradicting any statement contained in this Agreement or the Statement of Facts, provided however, that CFC may avail itself of any legal or factual arguments available to it in defending litigation regarding any matter discussed therein. Any such contradictory statement by CFC, its attorneys, board of directors, agents, officers, employees, or any other representative shall constitute a breach pursuant to paragraph 15 of this Agreement, and CFC would thereafter be subject to prosecution pursuant to the terms of this Agreement. The decision whether CFC has breached this Agreement based upon any statement by any person described in this paragraph which contradicts any information contained in the Statement of Facts shall be in the sole discretion of the Office. If and when the Office notifies CFC of a public statement by any such person that in whole or in part contradicts any part of the Statement of Facts, CFC may avoid breach of this Agreement by publicly repudiating such statement within forty-eight (48) hours after notification by the Office. Paragraph 15 sets forth the terms and conditions applicable to any breach of this Agreement by CFC.

Breach of Agreement

15. Should the Office, in its sole discretion, determine during the term of this Agreement that CFC has committed any federal crime commenced subsequent to the date of this Agreement, CFC shall thereafter be subject to prosecution for any federal crimes of which the Office has knowledge. Except in the event of a willful and material breach of this Agreement, it is the intention of the parties to this Agreement that all criminal and regulatory investigations arising from CFC's conduct or the facts contained in or involving the persons and/or accounts described in this Agreement and its exhibit, including the Statement of Facts, that have been or could have been conducted by the United States prior to the date of this Agreement shall not be pursued further against CFC.

16. Should the Office, in its sole discretion, determine that CFC has committed a willful and material breach of any provision of this Agreement, the Office shall provide written notice to CFC of the alleged breach and provide CFC with a two-week period in which to make a presentation to the Office to demonstrate that no breach has occurred or, to the extent applicable, that the breach is not willful or material or has been cured. The parties hereto expressly understand and agree that should CFC fail to make a presentation to the Office within the said two-week period, it shall be conclusively presumed that CFC is in willful and material breach of this Agreement. The parties further understand and agree that the Office's exercise of discretion under this paragraph is not subject to review in any court or tribunal.

17. Should the Office, in its sole discretion, determine that CFC has committed a willful and material breach of any provision of this Agreement, any such prosecutions that are not time- barred by the applicable statute of limitations on the date of the execution of this Agreement may be commenced against CFC. In addition, CFC agrees to toll, and exclude from any calculation of time, the running of the criminal statute of limitations for a period of two years from the date of

the execution of this Agreement and during any extension of the Deferred Prosecution period up to five years.

Sale or Merger

18. CFC agrees that if it sells or merges all or substantially all of its business operations as they exist as of the date of this Agreement, it shall include in any contract for sale or merger a provision binding the purchaser/successor to the obligations described in this Agreement.

Agreement's Limitations

19. It is further understood that this Agreement is binding on CFC and the United States, but specifically does not bind any other federal agencies, or any state or local authorities, although the United States will bring the cooperation of CFC and its compliance with its other obligations under this Agreement to the attention of the state or local prosecuting offices or any state or federal regulatory agencies, if requested by CFC or its attorneys.

20. It is further understood that this Agreement does not relate to or cover any criminal conduct by CFC other than the conduct described in, or arising from the facts contained in or involving the person and/or accounts described in, the Agreement and the Statement of Facts.

21. The Office may continue to investigate current and former CFC trustees, directors, officers, employees, consultants, agents, or attorneys. Nothing in this Agreement shall be construed to restrict in any way the ability of the Office and its designated agencies to investigate and prosecute any current or former CFC trustee, director, officer, employee, consultant, agent or attorney.

22. CFC and the Office agree that, upon acceptance by the Court, this Agreement and a proposed Order deferring prosecution shall be filed in the Office. CFC and the Office further agree that Appendix A of this Agreement will be filed under seal and shall remain under seal. CFC and the Office further agree that the information contained in Appendix A may be revealed at some point in time when and if CFC is finally determined to be in material breach of this Agreement.

Complete Agreement

23. This Agreement sets forth all the terms of the agreement between CFC and the Office. No amendment, modifications, or additions to this Agreement shall be valid unless they are in writing and signed by the office, the attorney(s) for CFC, and a duly authorized representative of CFC.

AGREED:

FOR CITRUS FLORIDA COMMUNITY COMPANY:

By: ______________________
Tomi Bell
Counsel for CFC
December __,
YEAR-1

FOR THE UNITED STATES OF AMERICA:

By: ______________________
Jo Jones
Assistant United States Attorney
December __, YEAR-1

Attachment U

APPENDIX A: STATEMENT OF FACTS

The following Statement of Facts is incorporated by reference as a part of the deferred prosecution agreement (the "Agreement") between the U.S. Attorney's Office for the Middle District of Florida ("Office") and Citrus Florida Community Company ("CFC").

1. CFC is a public company on the New York Stock Exchange and is organized, licensed and doing business under the laws of the United States. It employs eight-thousand (8,000) people.

2. CFC was founded in 1895 as a small citrus processing entity. Over the decades, the company expanded into all areas of the citrus industry, including the production of their own orange juice brands, among other things. CFC distributes its products to numerous national store chains and ships its products worldwide.

3. CFC's corporate headquarters are located in Tampa, Florida, with approximately one-hundred and fifty (150) people working at that location. CFC also has a cleaning supply processing and packaging plant that employs six-hundred (600) people located in Georgia. CFC also maintains a two-person office in New York to handle the shipments made throughout the Northeast.

4. Chief Executive Officer Jody Murray, General Counsel Cory Campbell, Head of Corporate Compliance and Human Resources Lynn Smith, Chief Operating Officer Kim Vanguard, Ashley Alden, Chris Smart, and Jess Henley, all work at CFC's corporate headquarters. Logan Walter formerly worked at CFC's corporate headquarters and reported to Chris Smart.

5. CFC also has a research and development facility located in Gulfport, Florida, approximately fifteen (15) miles away from the Tampa headquarters. This facility is headed by Dr. Sami Myers and contains about fifty (50) employees. Dr. Myers reports to Kim Vanguard.

6. Ashley Alden heads CFC's product distribution division, a group charged with marketing and selling new products to CFC's customers.

7. Chris Smart reports to Ashley Alden and leads a team that works on marketing initiatives.

8. Jess Henley also reports to Ashley Alden and leads a team that works on sales.

9. On or about June 1, YEAR-2 CFC began testing a new additive to be added to one of its orange juice brands. This additive was called "AOA." AOA was intended to achieve two results (1) it was expected to prolong the length of time the orange juice could remain on the shelf at retail establishments and (2) it was expected to make the orange juice taste fresher when consumed.

10. The initial testing of AOA was positive. Based on those positive results, Ashley Alden and Chris Smart began marketing the new orange juice and ordered new orange juice containers with the label "AOA" affixed.

11. On or about October 12, YEAR-2, Dr. Sami Myers called Ashley Alden to alert them of the final results for AOA. Dr. Myers disclosed that AOA did not work because it had no impact on the longevity or freshness of the orange juice.

12. Ashley Alden and Chris Smart did not change their marketing strategy in the wake of this information. The orange juice was launched as planned.

13. In March YEAR-1, Logan Walter met with the head of corporate compliance, Lynn Smith, and informed Lynn Smith of the conversation between Dr. Meyers, Ashley Alden and Chris Smart that Logan Walter overheard on October 12, YEAR-2.

14. Lynn Smith conducted an internal investigation. Over the course of the investigation, Lynn Smith was given the final test results that showed AOA was ineffective. Smith turned the final test results over to Cory Campbell, CFC's corporate counsel.

15. Cory Campbell shredded these final test results, making the results impossible to recover in the event of a government investigation.

16. On or about October 26, YEAR-2, Alden announced at a press conference that, among other things, the final test results show the AOA additive is effective. This statement was fraudulently made over the wires, resulting in a violation of Title 18, United States Code, Section 1343.

17. This statement was a violation of the above statute because: (1) CFC, or an agent thereof, used a scheme to defraud the shareholders of CFC and the public, (2) it was done in order to obtain money from an increase in the price of CFC shares, (3) the statement was made intentionally, (4) the statement was material, and (5) a CFC employee, Ashley Alden, used an interstate transmission to perpetuate the fraud.

18. The Office believes that at least three CFC employees executed their stock options based on non-public, inside information, in violation of the Securities and Exchange Act of 1934, Title 15, United States Code, Section 10(b).

IN THE UNITED STATES DISTRICT COURT
MIDDLE DISTRICT OF FLORIDA TAMPA
DIVISION

UNITED STATES OF AMERICA, Plaintiff, v. SAMI MYERS, Defendant.	)))))))	Case No. PLEA AGREEMENT

PLEA AGREEMENT

1. This Plea Agreement between the United States Attorney for the Middle District of Florida, and Defendant, Sami Myers, is made pursuant to Rule 11 of the Federal Rules of Criminal Procedure. The parties to this Agreement have agreed upon the following:

Charge in This Case

2. The Information in this case charges Defendant with mail fraud in violation of Title 18, United States Code, Section 1341.
3. Defendant has read the charge contained in the Information, and that charge has been fully explained by Defendant's attorney.
4. Defendant fully understands the nature and elements of the crime with which defendant is charged.

Charge to Which Defendant is Pleading Guilty

5. By this Plea Agreement, Defendant agrees to enter a voluntary plea of guilty to the Information, which charges Defendant with mail fraud, in violation of Title 18, United States Code, Section 1341. Defendant, Sami Myers, hereby waives the right to indictment by a grand jury and agrees to plead guilty to the Information in this case.

Factual Basis for Offense Charged

6. In pleading guilty, Defendant admits the following facts and that those facts establish defendant's guilt beyond a reasonable doubt, and establish a basis for this Plea Agreement:

   The Citrus Florida Community Company ("CFC"), Defendant's employer, is an international company that produces, distributes, and ships goods substantially impacting interstate commerce here in the United States. In addition to other products, CFC produces, distributes, and ships in interstate commerce orange juice, orange cleaning supplies, and orange based air fresheners. CFC owns and operates processing plants throughout the Southeast. Sami Myers is the head researcher and supervisor of the research and development facility for CFC and is located in an office in Gulfport, FL.

   From at least as early as October 12, YEAR-2, CFC began testing an orange juice additive known as AOA. AOA was designed by CFC to extend the shelf life of CFC's orange juice product thereby increasing the time the product would remain fresh before spoiling. Defendant cooperated with others in knowingly distributing false information about the effectiveness of the AOA orange juice additive, while charging customers a higher price, perpetuating mail fraud. Defendant, along with at least four others, released this information during a press conference, and allowed for customers to purchase stock in CFC via mail, telephone and internet. The business activities of Defendant and co-participants in connection with the sale of stock and purchase of orange juice affected were within the flow of, and substantially affected, interstate commerce.

Maximum Statutory Penalties

7. Defendant understands that the statutory maximum penalty which may be imposed against him upon conviction for violation of Title 18, United States Code, Section 1341 is as follows: (a) a term of imprisonment of up to twenty (20) years; (b) a fine up to $250,000; (c) a term of supervised release of three (3) years following any term of imprisonment and a violation of any condition of supervised release could result in imprisonment of up to two (2) years; (d) restitution to victims; and (e) a special assessment of $100 upon conviction.

8. Defendant understands that while determining the applicable Sentencing Guidelines range, the Court may consider conduct for which Defendant was not charged.
9. Defendant understands and acknowledges that no part of this Plea Agreement stipulates as to the actual sentence to be imposed.

Waiver of Constitutional Rights

10. Defendant, Sami Myers, understands and acknowledges that by pleading guilty to one (1) count of mail fraud pursuant to Title 18, United States Code, Section 1341, defendant hereby gives up the following rights as part of this Agreement:
    a) The right to plead not guilty to any criminal charges brought against them.
    b) The right to a speedy and public trial by jury.
    c) The right to the assistance of legal counsel at trial.
    d) The right to confront and cross-examine witnesses against defendant.
    e) The right to testify or to remain silent at trial.
    f) The right to present evidence in opposition to the offense charged, including calling witnesses and subpoenaing witnesses to testify.
    g) The right to be presumed innocent and to have the burden of proof placed on the government to prove each essential element of the charged offense beyond a reasonable doubt.
    h) The right to pursue any affirmative defenses, Fourth Amendment or Fifth Amendment constitutional challenges, and other pretrial motions that have been filed, or may be filed in this Court.
    i) Any right to appeal the imposition of the sentence against them.
    j) The right to any defenses based on statute of limitations.
    k) The right to any defenses based on improper jurisdiction.

Waiver of Appellate and Collateral Rights

11. Defendant understands that by pleading guilty and accepting this Plea Agreement, Defendant, Sami Myers, hereby waives the following rights:
    a) Any right Defendant may have under Title 18, United States Code, Section 3742 to appeal the sentence, including any restitution order imposed; and

b) Any right Defendant may have under Title 28, United States Code, Section 2255.

12. This Agreement shall in no way be construed as a waiver or forfeiture of Defendant's right to appeal based on a claim that Defendant's guilty plea was produced through coercion, force, or otherwise involuntarily made. Further, Defendant reserves the right to appeal any punishment in excess of the statutory maximum.

Waiver of Discovery Rights and Right to Brady Materials

13. Defendant understands and acknowledges that this Agreement requires Defendant to waive all rights to discovery. Further, Defendant understands that this Agreement requires Defendant to waive all rights to exculpatory or impeachment Brady material that might otherwise be available pursuant to Brady v. Maryland.

Cooperation

14. Defendant, Sami Myers, agrees to cooperate fully with the Office of the United States Attorney, and any other government body or agency, by providing accurate, complete and truthful information regarding Defendant's knowledge of any and all criminal activity, whether undertaken by Defendant or others, in any way involving or related to the AOA additive scheme described within this Plea Agreement. Defendant agrees to provide the Office of the United States Attorney and the government, with all documents and evidence within Defendant's possession, or whose whereabouts are known to Defendant, related to this criminal investigation. It is an expressed condition of this Agreement that Defendant must, at all times, give accurate, complete, and truthful information and testimony. Defendant may not withhold information from the government or refuse to testify truthfully and completely. Defendant must attend all meetings, interviews, court appearances, and must timely provide all requested documents and records.

15. In exchange for Defendant's plea of guilty to one (1) count of mail fraud, and full cooperation as detailed in this Agreement, the Office of the United States Attorney for the Middle District of Florida will not prosecute Defendant, Dr. Sami Myers, for any other federal criminal offenses committed in the Middle District of Florida in any way involving or related to the AOA additive scheme described within this Plea Agreement,

which was committed by Defendant up to the date of the execution of this Plea Agreement, and about which Defendant provides complete and truthful information.

16. The Office of the United States Attorney and Defendant agree that this Plea Agreement is not contingent upon the government filing charges against, the return of an Indictment against, or the successful prosecution of, any person or the CFC Company.

17. If the Office of the United States Attorney determines that Defendant has provided substantial assistance in an investigation or prosecution of others, and if Defendant has fully complied with all of the obligations under this Agreement, the United States will make a motion, pursuant to U.S.S.G. § 5K1.1, requesting the Court to sentence Defendant in light of the advisory factors set forth in § 5K1.1(a)(1)-(5).

18. For purposes of determining Defendant's cooperation, the Office of the United States Attorney for the Middle District of Florida shall have the sole responsibility for determining whether or not defendant's cooperation has been accurate, complete, and truthful.

Government's Obligations

19. If Defendant, Sami Myers, complies fully with all defendants' obligations under this Plea Agreement, the Office of the United States Attorney for the Middle District of Florida agrees to:

    a) Not prosecute Defendant, Sami Myers, for any other violations of federal criminal law it committed in the Middle District of Florida in any way involving or related to the AOA additive scheme described throughout this Plea Agreement. This agreement to not prosecute is limited to those violations of federal criminal law committed before execution of this Agreement and about which Defendant provides accurate, complete and truthful information to the government. The non-prosecution terms contained in this paragraph do not apply to civil actions of any kind.

    b) Not dispute facts agreed to in this Agreement.

    c) Not publicly disclose any confidential information contained in this Agreement, except as may be necessary to investigate and prosecute possible violations of federal criminal law.

d) Follow all stipulations contained in this Agreement.

Breach of the Plea Agreement

20. Defendant understands that if the Office of the United States Attorney determines that Defendant breached this Plea Agreement, the government may prosecute Defendant for all offenses for which the United States has evidence. If Defendant breaches this Agreement, or is found to have violated any portion of this Agreement, Defendant waives any objection or legal challenge it may have, to the re-institution of any charges in the Indictment that were previously dismissed by this Court, or any additional charges that had not been charged or prosecuted by the government.
21. Defendant agrees that, in the event that the United States is released from its obligations under this Plea Agreement and brings criminal charges against Defendant for any relevant offense, the statute of limitations period for such offense will be tolled for the period between the date of the signing of this Plea Agreement and six (6) months after the date the United States gave notice of its intent to void its obligations under this Plea Agreement.
22. Defendant understands and agrees that in any further prosecution of Defendant resulting from the release of the United States from its obligations under this Plea Agreement based on Defendant's violation of the Plea Agreement, any documents, statements, information, testimony, or evidence provided by Defendant to attorneys or agents of the United States, federal grand juries, or courts, and any leads derived therefrom, may be used against Defendant in any such further prosecution. In addition, Defendant unconditionally waives the right to challenge the use of such evidence in any such further prosecution, notwithstanding Fed. R. Evid. 410.

Agreement Not Binding on Other Jurisdictions and Agencies

23. Defendant understands and acknowledges that this Agreement binds only the Office of the United States Attorney for the Middle District of Florida. Defendant understands that this Agreement does not bind any other federal, state, local, administrative, regulatory, or other governmental body or agency with prosecuting authority.

Defendant's Counsel and Waiver of Ineffective Assistance of Counsel Claims

24. Defendant acknowledges receiving the assistance of counsel from attorney Dakota Holt concerning this Plea Agreement and the underlying charges as detailed throughout this Agreement. Defendant is satisfied with the legal services and advice provided by Dakota Holt and waives any later claims of ineffective assistance of counsel.

Voluntariness of Plea

25. Defendant has freely and voluntarily entered into this Agreement. Defendant further agrees that no threats, representations, or promises, other than promises contained in this plea Agreement, were made to induce or entice defendant to enter this plea of guilty and to accept this Agreement.

Entirety of Agreement

26. This Plea Agreement constitutes the entire agreement between the United States and Defendant concerning the disposition of the criminal charge in this case. This Plea Agreement cannot be modified except in writing, signed by the United States and Defendant.

Dated this _____ day of December, YEAR-1.

____
SAMI MYERS
Defendant

____
DAKOTA HOLT
Attorney for Defendant

____
JO JONES
Assistant United States Attorney

UNITED STATES DISTRICT COURT
MIDDLE DISTRICT OF FLORIDA
TAMPA DIVISION

UNITED STATES OF AMERICA

v.		Case No.	8:11-cr-XXXX
			15 U.S.C. § 78ff
JODY MURRAY			15 U.S.C. § 78j
CORY CAMPBELL			15 U.S.C. § 78p
SAMI MYERS			18 U.S.C. § 2
JESS HENLEY			18 U.S.C. § 1341
ASHLEY ALDEN and			18 U.S.C. § 1343
CHRIS SMART			18 U.S.C. § 1346
			18 U.S.C. § 1505
			17 C.F.R. § 240.10b-5

INDICTMENT

The Grand Jury charges:

Introduction

At times material to this Indictment:

1. Citrus Florida Community Company (hereinafter, "CFC") is a publicly held company on the New York Stock Exchange, doing business and servicing many areas of the nation including areas within the Middle District of Florida, with citrus based products. Corporate headquarters for CFC is located in Tampa, Florida within the Middle District

of Florida.

2. JODY MURRAY, CORY CAMPBELL, ASHLEY ALDEN, JESS HENLEY, and CHRIS SMART, are employed at CFC's headquarters located in Tampa, Florida.

3. JODY MURRAY is CFC's Chief Executive Officer and Chairperson of the Board of Directors.

4. CORY CAMPBELL is CFC's General Counsel.

5. ASHLEY ALDEN is CFC's Head of the Product Distribution Division.

6. JESS HENLEY is CFC's Head of the Sales Team.

7. CHRIS SMART is CFC's Head of the Marketing Team.

8. CFC operates a research and development division, headed by SAMI MYERS, in Gulfport, Florida in the Middle District of Florida.

9. SAMI MYERS' principle work was in the testing of the experimental orange juice additive AOA.

10. On or about October 12, YEAR-2, Dr. SAMI MYERS had a telephone conference with JESS HENLEY, ASHLEY ALDEN, and CHRIS SMART, in which they conspired to destroy an unfavorable test report regarding the AOA additive.

11. It was further a part of the conspiracy that the conspirators would continue to represent AOA as though it were effective.

12. It was further a part of the conspiracy that the conspirators would benefit from the rise in value of the CFC stock, and have the opportunity to sell their stock options at a higher price.

13. On October 26, YEAR-2, ASHLEY ALDEN made statements they knew to be false representations about the effectiveness of AOA to the press and investors, causing CFC stock to rise in value.

14. CFC conducted an internal investigation and informed JODY MURRAY of the conspirators' actions.

15. CORY CAMPBELL concealed the conspiracy and shredded the results of SAMI MYERS' research, which concluded that AOA was ineffective, thus aiding in the concealment of the fraud.

16. Jody MURRAY utilized e-mail to further the fraud by concealing the behavior. MURRAY also concealed the fraud perpetrated by the conspirators by rewarding them with corporate bonuses for "Outstanding Company Work."

Count One
(Honest Services Mail Fraud)
18 U.S.C. §§ 1341, 1346

17. The allegations contained in Paragraph 1 through 16 of this Indictment are incorporated by reference as though fully set forth herein.

18. Beginning on or about October 12, YEAR-2, and continuing until in or around April YEAR-1, in the Middle District of Florida and elsewhere,

SAMI MYERS,
JESS HENLEY,
ASHLEY ALDEN,
and
CHRIS SMART,

Defendants herein, and other persons known and unknown to the Grand Jury, devised and intended to devise a scheme and artifice to defraud and for obtaining money and property by means of materially false and fraudulent pretenses, representations, and promises, and to deprive the citizens of the Middle District of Florida and elsewhere, of their right to the honest services of the defendants and CFC, by utilizing the mails or interstate carrier in violation of Title 18, United States Code, Sections 1341 and 1346.

Count Two
(Conspiracy to Commit Honest Services Mail Fraud)
18 U.S.C. §§ 1341 and 1346

19. The allegations contained in Paragraph 1 through 16 of this Indictment are incorporated by reference as though fully set forth herein.

20. From in or about October 12, YEAR-2, and continuing through April YEAR-1, within the Middle District of Florida and elsewhere,

SAMI MYERS,
JESS HENLEY,
ASHLEY ALDEN,
and
CHRIS SMART,

the defendants herein, did unlawfully, knowingly and willfully combine, conspire, and agree with each other and with others, both known and unknown to the Grand Jury, to devise and intend to devise a scheme and artifice to defraud and for obtaining money and property by means of materially false and fraudulent pretenses, representations, and promises, and to deprive the citizens of the Middle District of Florida, and elsewhere of their right to the honest services of the defendants and CFC, utilizing mails or interstate carrier in violation of Title 18, United States Code, Sections 1341 and 1346.

<u>Count Three</u>
(Securities Fraud)
15 U.S.C. §§ 78j(b) and 78ff;
17 C.F.R., § 240.10b-5; and
18 U.S.C. § 2

21. The allegations contained in Paragraph 1 through 16 of this Indictment are incorporated by reference as though fully set forth herein.

22. On or about October 12, YEAR-2, and continuing through about December YEAR-2, within the Middle District of Florida and elsewhere,

SAMI MYERS,
JESS HENLEY,
ASHLEY ALDEN,
and
CHRIS SMART,

Unlawfully, willfully, and knowingly, directly and indirectly, by use of the means and instrumentalities of interstate commerce, the mails and the facilities of national securities exchanges, did use and employ manipulative and deceptive devices and contrivances, in violation of Title 17, Code of Federal Regulations, Section 240.10b-5, by (a) employing devices, schemes, and artifices to defraud; (b) making untrue statements of material facts and omitting to state material facts necessary in order to make the statements made, in the light of the circumstances under which they were made, not misleading; and (c) engaging in acts, practices and courses of business which operated and would operate as a fraud and deceit upon purchasers and sellers of CFC common stock, all in violation of 15 U.S.C. §§ 78j(b) and 78ff; and 18 U.S.C. § 2.

23. On October 27, YEAR-2, SAMI MYERS, ASHLEY ALDEN, and CHRIS SMART executed their stock options and sold a significant amount of their CFC stock. JESS HENLEY's Stock Option value increased from $28 per share to $34 per share.

Count Four
(Insider Trading)
15 U.S.C. §§ 78p and 78j(c)(1);
17 C.F.R. § 240.10b-5(c); and
18 U.S.C. § 2

24. The allegations contained in Paragraph 1 through 16 of this Indictment are incorporated by reference as though fully set forth herein.

25. On or about October 12, YEAR-2, and continuing through about October 27, YEAR-1, within the Middle District of Florida and elsewhere,

SAMI MYERS,
JESS HENLEY,
ASHLEY ALDEN,
and
CHRIS SMART,

Unlawfully, willfully, and knowingly, directly and indirectly, by use of the means and instrumentalities of interstate commerce, the mails and the facilities of national securities exchanges, did effect, accept, or facilitate a transaction involving the loan or borrowing of securities in contravention of such rules and regulations as the Commission may prescribe as necessary or appropriate in the public interest or for the protection of investors. Specifically, the defendants engaged in the sale or trade of CFC common stock, while acting as an officer, director or principal stockholder under the definition of Title 15, United States Code, Section 78p(a)(1), in violation of Title 15, United States Code, Section 78j(c)(1); Title 17, Code of Federal Regulations, Section 240.10b-5(c); and Title 18, United States Code, Section 2.

Count Five
(Obstruction of Justice)
18 U.S.C. §§ 1505 and 2

26. The allegations contained in Paragraph 1 through 16 of this Indictment are incorporated by reference as though fully set forth herein.

27. On or about October 12, YEAR-2, and continuing through around December YEAR-1, in the Middle District of Florida,

CORY CAMPBELL

defendant herein, did corruptly endeavor to avoid, evade, prevent, influence, obstruct and impede the due and proper administration of the law under which the pending proceedings were being had before the Securities and Exchange Commission, the Food and Drug Administration, and the United States Attorney's Office of both the Southern District of New York and the Middle District of Florida, all departments or agencies of the United State. Specifically, the defendant destroyed or caused to be destroyed documentary material, which was the subject of the investigation or proceeding before the listed departments or agencies of the United States government; in violation of Title 18, United States Code, Sections 1505 and 2.

Count Six
(Obstruction of Justice)
18 U.S.C. §§ 1505 and 2

28. The allegations contained in Paragraph 1 through 16 of this Indictment are incorporated by reference as though fully set forth herein.

29. ASHLEY ALDEN possessed a diary that contained relevant and material information concerning the AOA conspiracy.

30. ASHLEY ALDEN destroyed the diary after receiving a subpoena related to the investigation of the offenses outlined in this Indictment.

31. On or about October 12, YEAR-2, and continuing through around December YEAR-1, in the Middle District of Florida,

ASHLEY ALDEN

defendant herein, did corruptly endeavor to avoid, evade, prevent, influence, obstruct and impede the due and proper administration of the law under which the pending proceedings were being had before the Securities and Exchange Commission, the Food and Drug Administration, and the United States Attorney's Office of both the Southern District of New York and the Middle District of Florida, all departments or agencies of the United State. Specifically, the defendant destroyed or caused to be destroyed documentary material, which was the subject of to the investigation or proceeding before the listed departments or agencies of the United States government; in violation of Title 18, United States Code, Sections 1505 and 2.

Count Seven
(Honest Services Wire Fraud)
18 U.S.C. §§ 1343, 1346

32. The allegations contained in Paragraph 1 through 16 of this Indictment are incorporated by reference as though fully set forth herein.

33. Beginning on or about October 12, YEAR-2, and continuing until in or around April YEAR-1, in the Middle District of Florida and elsewhere,

CORY CAMPBELL
JODY MURRAY

Defendants herein, and other persons known and unknown to the Grand Jury, devised and intended to devise a scheme and artifice to defraud and for obtaining money and property by means of materially false and fraudulent pretenses, representations, and promises, and to deprive the citizens of the Middle District of Florida and elsewhere, of their right to the honest services of the defendants and CFC, by utilizing transmissions via wire and radio communication in interstate and foreign commerce of any writings, signs, signals, pictures and sounds, in violation of Title 18, United States Code, Sections 1343, 1346, and 2.

A TRUE BILL,

G. Johnson

Foreperson
Dated December 15, YEAR-1

United States Attorney

By:

Jo Jones

JO JONES
Assistant United States Attorney

Attachment W

JOINT DEFENSE AGREEMENT

THIS JOINT DEFENSE AGREEMENT (the "Agreement") is entered into by and among the undersigned Counsel, as of January 10, YEAR-0, acting for and on behalf of their respective clients ("the Parties"), each of whom is a defendant having been indicted in Case No. 9:11-cr- XXXX in the Middle District of Florida. Counsel believes that the Parties share a common interest in the defense of these alleged crimes and wish to continue to pursue their separate but common interests and to avoid any suggestion of waiver of the confidentiality of privileged communications or documents. They hereby agree as follows:

1. The Parties and their Counsel believe that it is in their individual and mutual interests to share certain information related to their investigation and defense of the charges against their clients. These communications may include but are not limited to written communications, the disclosure of documents, factual and legal analyses, summaries, and memoranda, opinions, legal strategies, interview reports and reports of experts, consultants or investigators, joint meetings between defense counsel, the parties, their representatives and employees, and any meetings with prospective witnesses or consulting experts or litigation support service providers in connection with the litigation in person, by telephone or in any other form, and records or reports of such communications.

2. Nothing in this Agreement shall be construed to affect the separate and independent representation of each client by his or her respective Counsel.

3. Some or all of the Defense Materials may be protected from disclosure to adverse or other Parties as a result of the attorney-client privilege, the work product doctrine, or other applicable privileges, protections or immunities. It is the desire, intention, and mutual understanding of the Parties hereto (a) that the sharing of Defense Materials among one another is not intended to, and shall not, waive or diminish in any way the confidentiality of such materials or their continued protection under the attorney-client privilege, the work product doctrine or other applicable privileges, protections or immunities; and (b) that all Defense Materials provided by a Counsel or the Parties pursuant to this Agreement that are entitled to protection under the attorney-client privilege, the work product doctrine or other applicable privileges, protections or immunities, shall remain entitled to such protection under the common interest doctrine, and may not be disclosed to persons other than those described in Paragraph 6 without the consent of the providing party. The Parties also intend and understand that any disclosure of Defense Materials pursuant to this Agreement will not constitute a waiver of any available privilege, protection or immunity.

4. The Parties and their Counsel agree not to disclose to any other person or entity privileged information received after the date of this Agreement from another party or counsel unless the Parties or Counsel wishing to disclose the information first obtains the consent of Counsel for all other Parties who may be entitled to claim any

privilege or protection with respect to such information, except to the extent explicitly permitted pursuant to a different section of this Agreement.

5. In the event any Party or Counsel to this Agreement enters into a debriefing, plea, or other cooperative agreement with the government, that Signatory agrees to disclose in any and all agreements that they are bound by a joint defense agreement and that they are prohibited from disclosing information obtained pursuant to that Agreement. All written agreements entered into between the government and that Signatory shall contain the following: "Nothing in this Agreement is intended to abrogate any joint defense relationship or privilege that may exist between defendant and any other individual."

6. Each of the undersigned Counsel has further agreed that they will not disclose any exchanged Defense Materials received by them from another Party to this Agreement or Counsel for another Party to this Agreement to anyone except paralegals, support staff, or experts who are directly employed by or retained by and assisting Counsel in the defense of these alleged crimes. All persons permitted access to Defense Materials (collectively, "Authorized Persons") shall be specifically advised that the Defense Materials are privileged and subject to the terms of this Agreement.

7. Any shared Defense Materials, and the information contained therein, are to be used by each person or Party receiving them solely in connection with the defense of the crimes. Neither the Defense Materials nor the information contained therein may be used by any person or Party receiving them for any other purpose whatsoever.

8. All Defense Materials exchanged between and among any of the undersigned counsel pursuant to prior oral agreements or any previous joint defense agreement are now subject to this Agreement. This Agreement specifically preserves the protections afforded to those materials shared between the parties from the time that the commonality of interest came into being until execution of this Agreement under the same terms as contained in this Agreement.

9. The privileges and protections for the Defense Materials to which this Agreement is applicable may not be waived by any Party to this Agreement without the prior written consent of the Party that provided the Defense Materials. Any inadvertent or purposeful disclosure of Defense Materials exchanged pursuant to this Agreement that is made by a Party contrary to the terms of this Agreement shall not constitute a waiver of any privilege or protection. If any Party is required by court order or rule of law to produce or reveal any confidential information, documents or privileged materials which are part of the Parties' efforts pursuant to this Agreement, reasonable notice shall be given to each Party who has executed this Agreement before responding to, or complying with, such requests so that any Party may, at its own cost, have the opportunity to resist the production of such information by timely and appropriate process. In the event the Party from whom disclosure is sought has

no objection to the disclosure, such Party shall nevertheless invoke this Agreement during the pendency of any action taken by the objecting Party and shall otherwise make reasonable efforts to prevent disclosure until the final resolution of the objection of the objecting Party.

10. In the event that a Party determines that it no longer has a commonality of interest in the defense of the crimes, such Party shall withdraw from this Agreement. Each undersigned Counsel has a duty to withdraw from the Agreement when, in good faith, they reasonably believes that a commonality of interest no longer exists and to give prompt written notice of such withdrawal to each of the undersigned. Notwithstanding a Party's withdrawal, this Agreement shall remain operative as to: (a) all other remaining Parties to this Agreement; and (b) all previously furnished Defense Materials. Any Party may withdraw from this Agreement on written notice to all of the undersigned Counsel. Each Signatory agrees immediately to notify in writing all other Signatories when any Client or Counsel engages in discussions concerning possible cooperation with the government or when a Client decides to cooperate with the government, grant an interview, or make any form of proffer to the government either directly or through counsel. Any such withdrawal will be solely on a prospective basis and any Defense Materials provided pursuant to this Agreement prior to such withdrawal shall continue to be governed by the terms of this Agreement. Each Signatory specifically acknowledges that any Client may become a witness, whether voluntarily or otherwise, in connection with or as a result of the investigation. In the event that any Client becomes a witness, nothing in this Agreement shall create a conflict of interest so as to require the disqualification of any Counsel from the representation of their Client, based on the existence of this agreement or any sharing of Defense Materials. By entering into this Agreement, each Client and each Counsel knowingly and intelligently waives any conflict of interest or other objection that might otherwise be available based upon the sharing of information pursuant to this Agreement. Any Client who enters into a cooperation agreement with the government or who testifies in any civil, administrative, or criminal proceeding arising from this matter hereby consents to any other Signatory using for defense purposes any information or material contributed by the Client or their Counsel, and waives any conflict of interest related thereto. This Agreement specifically permits the use of contributed information or material in cross-examining the former joint defense participant and permits the presentation of the material or information by the defense at any point in the proceeding. Each Client further represents that they have consulted with their own Counsel regarding this provision and its implications and waives any conflicts of interest that might be created thereby. All materials that are exchanged pursuant to this Agreement shall be marked and identified as being provided with the following language: "Confidential and privileged communication produced pursuant to joint defense agreement." Any signatory withdrawing from the Agreement for any reason, or upon its termination, shall immediately return all copies of such materials to the producing party.

11. A party who is dismissed or settles all pending claims will be deemed to have withdrawn from the Agreement in accordance with terms of paragraph 10 as of the date of the dismissal or settlement.

12. The provisions of this Agreement may be modified only by written agreement of all affected Parties, and it shall be binding upon all successors and assigns of the Parties.

13. The parties recognize that other counsel and their clients may be permitted to join this Agreement at a future time by signing a copy of this Agreement. Any such additions shall be made only with the permission of all then-current Signatories to this Agreement.

14. While the undersigned believe that their clients are well served by the sharing of information under this Agreement, they also understand that participation in this Agreement represents neither an endorsement of, nor an authorization to control, the defense strategy or decisions of other participating counsels' clients.

15. Nothing in this Agreement shall relieve the Parties or their counsel from any obligation or obligations pursuant to the terms of any protective order or similar order entered by any court regarding the disclosure of dissemination of information pertaining to any crimes.

16. Nothing in this Agreement shall limit the right of any Party to use or disclose any documents or information or work product that have been independently obtained or generated by such Party (i.e. they were not obtained or generated as part of the common defense efforts made pursuant to this Agreement), whether or not such documents, information or work product have been provided to any other Party pursuant to this Agreement.

17. Nothing in this Agreement shall prevent the Parties from entering into joint defense agreements with other parties or among themselves, and this Agreement shall not be deemed to supersede or nullify, in whole or in part, any joint defense agreement any Party has entered into prior to the date of its execution of this Agreement.

18. This Agreement shall be interpreted so as to afford the broadest and greatest protection possible of Defense Materials from disclosure to third parties.

19. Nothing in this Agreement shall be construed to create an attorney-client relationship. Each Party represents and acknowledges that they are represented exclusively by their own Counsel. Each undersigned counsel understands that it is their sole responsibility to represent their or their respective client and that none of the other signatories to this Agreement have in any way assumed any such responsibility. Moreover, the participation in, execution or receipt of any information pursuant to this Agreement shall not disqualify any representative of a signatory

(including a law firm) from accepting any other future engagement. Nothing in this Agreement shall be construed to create an attorney-client relationship. Each Counsel participating in the Joint Defense Group is obligated to maintain the confidentiality of information as specified in the Agreement, but each Counsel does not act on behalf of any person other than their own Client.

20. Nothing in this Agreement is intended as, nor shall be construed or deemed to be, an admission of liability by any Party, or of the existence of facts upon which liability could be based.

21. This Agreement shall continue in full force and effect notwithstanding any conclusion or resolution as to any Party of the crimes.

22. The contents of this Agreement are confidential and shall not be released to any person or entity not a Party to this Agreement or as necessary to enforce the terms of this Agreement.

23. This Agreement may be signed in counterparts. All executed counterparts shall comprise the entire Agreement. This Agreement may be executed by counsel for a Party. Each counsel signing this Agreement represents that they have been authorized by their client to execute this Agreement on behalf of the client.

IN WITNESS WHEREOF, the Parties have executed this Agreement on the dates indicated below.

By:________________________	By:________________________
________________________	________________________
Counsel for Jody Myers	Counsel for Cory Campbell
Dated: _______________	Dated: _______________
By:________________________	By:________________________
________________________	________________________
Counsel for Sami Myers	Counsel for Jess Henley
Dated: _______________	Dated: _______________

By:______________________________

____
Counsel for Ashley Alden

Dated: ____________________

By:______________________________

____
Counsel for Chris Smart

Dated: ____________________

Attachment X

UNITED STATES DISTRICT COURT
MIDDLE DISTRICT OF FLORIDA
TAMPA DIVISION

UNITED STATES OF AMERICA   Case No. 8:11-cr-XXXX

v.

CHRIS SMART
JODY MURRAY
CORY CAMPBELL
SAMI MYERS
JESS HENLEY

DEFENDANTS' MOTION FOR DISCOVERY AND INSPECTION

COME NOW the Defendants, Jody Murray, Jess Henley, Sami Myers, Chris Smart and Cory Campbell, collectively by and through undersigned counsel and pursuant to Rule 16 of the Federal Rules of Criminal Procedure, respectfully moves the court to order the Government to produce for inspection and copying the following, which are known to, or are in the possession of, the Government or any of its agents, or which through due diligence would become known from the investigating officers or witnesses or persons having knowledge of this case:

1. A written summary of any testimony the government intends to use under Rule 702, 703, or 705 of the Federal Rules of Evidence during its case in chief. This summary must include the expert witnesses' opinions, the bases and reasons for those opinions, and the witness's qualifications.

2. Discovery of all documents and evidence described in Rule 16(a) of the Federal Rules of Criminal Procedure. Additionally, the defense specifically requests the following items:

Attachment Y

a. Any and all statements of defendants, including written and recorded statements, either to government agents or third parties irrespective of whether the Government intends to introduce them at trial.

b. Any and all statements of co-conspirators, including written and recorded statements, either to government agents or third parties irrespective of whether the Government intends to introduce them at trial.

c. Any and all statements of Government witnesses, including written and recorded statements, either to government agents or third parties irrespective of whether the Government intends to introduce them at trial.

d. Any and all statements made before any Grand Jury investigating this matter or any related matters.

e. Any and all tape recordings of telephone conversations or transcripts to which the Defendant or any alleged co-conspirator or witness is purported to be a party.

f. Any and all documents, instruments, or forms of any kind signed or purported to have been signed by the Defendant, co-conspirators or witnesses.

g. Any and all books, papers, documents, photographs, videotapes, computer storage devices, electronic materials or data, or tangible objects, which are in the possession, custody or control of the Government which are material to the preparation of Defendant's defense, including but not limited to, all currency, documents, instruments, or other writings obtained from the Defendant or witnesses.

h. Any and all reports prepared by any Government agency, including original notes used in preparation of these reports.

Attachment Y

3. The Defense requests an order to disclose and provide any forms of potential bias of prospective witnesses for the government, including, but not limited to: proffers, plea agreements, promises of leniency or immunity, incentives to curry favor with the IRS, SEC, or civil agreements, and any form of direct/indirect consideration, provided for or protected by the government that could encourage favorable testimony and be a possible source of witness bias or impair credibility. Additionally any and all documents, forms, summaries, rap sheets or other records or information reflecting the criminal record of any witness or person having knowledge of any matter relevant to this cause of action, whether or not said witness or person is to be called to testify at the time of trial. Additionally, the personnel files of each government agent that would reflect on the credibility of the agent witness or otherwise be favorable to the defense.

4. The names and addresses of any and all individuals whom the Government intends to call as witnesses either in its case-in-chief or as rebuttal witnesses and all individuals who were interviewed by the Government or its agents in connection with this case.

Respectfully submitted,

s/ ______________________

Counsel for the Defendants

CERTIFICATE OF SERVICE

I HEREBY CERTIFY that a true and correct copy of the foregoing was hand-delivered to the Office of the United States Attorney of the Middle District of Florida, 400 North Tampa Street Suite 3200, Tampa, Florida, this January 15, YEAR-0.

LAW OFFICE OF DAKOTA HOLT

ATTORNEY AT LAW

1 Holt Drive
Tampa, Florida 33629
www.dakotaholt.com

Telephone: (813) 555-5555
Facsimile: (813) 555-5556
Email: dakota@dakotaholt.com

ATTORNEY-CLIENT/WORK PRODUCT PRIVILEGE COMMUNICATION

January 20, YEAR-0

Mickey Miller
201 Miller Avenue
Tampa, Florida 33626

Re: Professional Engagement in Representation of Ashley Alden, Chris Smart, Jess Henley, Cory Campbell, Jody Murray, and Dr. Sami Myers

Dear Miller:

I have been authorized to retain your services in assisting the joint defense representation of Ashley Alden, Chris Smart, Jess Henley, Jody Murray, Cory Campbell, and Dr. Sami Myers in connection with the federal criminal proceedings in reference to the Central Florida Company's orange juice additive "AOA."

We are retaining your forensic accounting services to assist us in determining potential loss values should the government be successful in proving its case, as well as providing each individual defendant an assessment of their fraud loss.

The joint defense is engaging your services for the purposes of assisting us in representing the interests of our clients, Ashley Alden, Jody Murray, Cory Campbell, Chris Smart, Jess Henley, and Dr. Sami Myers. Your services are being specifically sought to aid us in providing advice to our clients and in anticipation of litigation or other related proceedings.

Accordingly, all actions taken by you or any other representative of your firm in assisting us in this representation comes within the purview of the attorney-client privilege, a privilege that belongs solely to the clients, Ashley Alden, Cory Campbell, Jody Murray, Chris Smart, Jess Henley, and Dr. Sami Myers. In addition, all communications to and from our firm are **PRIVILEGED AND CONFIDENTIAL**, and should be treated and identified as such in all communications. All written communications should be directed to our firm for appropriate dissemination, and again, should be appropriately captioned as privileged and confidential materials.

Attachment Z

Your bills should be directed to me for payment. Your fees will be based on actual hours expended at your standard rates, plus out-of-pocket costs. We agree to compensate you at the rate of $350 per hour. If we disagree with your fee payments as shown on any invoice, or with any of your services hereunder, we agree that any such dispute will be submitted for resolution by arbitration in accordance with the rules of the American Arbitration Association. Such arbitration shall be binding and final. In agreeing to arbitration, we both acknowledge that in the event of a dispute over fees or services, each of us is giving up the right to have the dispute decided in a court of law before a judge or jury and instead are accepting the use of arbitration for resolution.

Any written reports or other documents which you prepare in connection with this engagement are to be used only for the purpose of this matter and may not be published or used for any other purpose without our prior written consent.

Any party may terminate this agreement effective upon written notice to the other parties. In such case, our Client shall pay your fees and costs incurred through the effective date of such termination.

By fully executing a duplicate original of this letter and sending it to us, you are confirming that the terms of this letter became effective as of the first date you render services in connection with this engagement. In this regard, any invoice presented by you that includes such billings is due and payable upon presentation of the invoice.

Thank you for your willingness to assist us in this matter, and we truly look forward to working with you. Should you have any questions, please feel free to call at any time.

Sincerely,

Dakota Holt

Dakota Holt
Attorney for Dr. Sami Myers

cc: Attorney for Ashley Alden
Attorney for Chris Smart
Attorney for Jess Henley
Attorney for Cory Campbell
Attorney for Jody Murray

Approved as to the engagement and fees by:

____
Mickey Miller

Date ____________________________

Attachment Z

LAW OFFICE OF DAKOTA HOLT

ATTORNEY AT LAW

1 Holt Drive
Tampa, Florida 33629
www.dakotaholt.com

Telephone: (813) 555-5555
Facsimile: (813) 555-5556
Email: dakota@dakotaholt.com

ATTORNEY-CLIENT/WORK PRODUCT PRIVILEGE COMMUNICATION

January 20, YEAR-0

Professor Amari Andersen
California Institute of Technology
1200 East California Blvd.
Pasadena, CA 91125

Re: Professional Engagement in Representation of Ashley Alden, Chris Smart, Jess Henley, Cory Campbell, Jody Murray, and Dr. Sami Myers

Dear Professor Andersen:

I have been authorized to retain your services in assisting the joint defense representation of Ashley Alden, Chris Smart, Jess Henley, Jody Murray, Cory Campbell, and Dr. Sami Myers in connection with the federal criminal proceedings in reference to the Central Florida Company's orange juice additive "AOA."

We are retaining you as a consultant as a result of your extensive studies in extending the longevity in liquid products. You may be asked to provide expert witness services and testimony in this matter should it become necessary. Therefore you agree to maintain the confidentiality of all information and documentation received during this work and will abide by all court orders regarding the disclosure of information relating to this matter. We understand you do not warrant or predict the development or outcome of this matter and your fees are not contingent on the results.

The joint defense is engaging your services for the purposes of assisting us in representing the interests of our clients, Ashley Alden, Jody Murray, Cory Campbell, Chris Smart, Jess Henley, and Dr. Sami Myers. Your services are being specifically sought to aid us in providing advice to our clients and in anticipation of litigation or other related proceedings.

Accordingly, all actions taken by you or any other representative of your firm in assisting us in this representation comes within the purview of the attorney-client privilege, a privilege that belongs solely to the clients, Ashley Alden, Cory Campbell, Jody Murray, Chris Smart, Jess Henley, and Dr. Sami Myers. In addition, all communications to and from our firm are **PRIVILEGED AND CONFIDENTIAL**, and should be treated and identified as such in all communications. All written communications should be directed to our firm for appropriate dissemination, and again, should be appropriately captioned as privileged and confidential materials.

Your bills should be directed to me for payment. Your fees will be based on actual hours expended at your standard rates, plus out-of-pocket costs. We agree to compensate you at the out-of-court rate of $300 per hour and in-court rate of $500 per hour. We understand occasionally you may use independent contractors to assist in our assignment subject to the same fee schedule. Fees, with costs, may be billed to our Client monthly during periods of activity on our behalf. Our Client may also be billed for out-of-pocket expenses such as delivery service, postage, telephone, travel, meals and lodging, photocopy, computer charges and other expenses, etc., and out-of-pocket expenses. If we disagree with your fee payments as shown on any invoice, or with any of your services hereunder, we agree that any such dispute will be submitted for resolution by arbitration in accordance with the rules of the American Arbitration Association. Such arbitration shall be binding and final. In agreeing to arbitration, we both acknowledge that in the event of a dispute over fees or services, each of us is giving up the right to have the dispute decided in a court of law before a judge or jury and instead are accepting the use of arbitration for resolution.

Any written reports or other documents which you prepare in connection with this engagement are to be used only for the purpose of this matter and may not be published or used for any other purpose without our prior written consent.

Any party may terminate this agreement effective upon written notice to the other parties. In such case, our Client shall pay your fees and costs incurred through the effective date of such termination.

By fully executing a duplicate original of this letter and sending it to us, you are confirming that the terms of this letter became effective as of the first date you render services in connection with this engagement. In this regard, any invoice presented by you that includes such billings is due and payable upon presentation of the invoice.

Thank you for your willingness to assist us in this matter, and we truly look forward to working with you. Should you have any questions, please feel free to call at any time.

Sincerely,

Dakota Holt
Attorney for Dr. Sami Myers

cc: Attorney for Ashley Alden
Attorney for Chris Smart
Attorney for Jess Henley
Attorney for Cory Campbell
Attorney for Jody Murray

Attachment AA

Approved as to the engagement and fees by:

____

Professor Amari Andersen

Date ________________________________

BEGPROONO : M-INT-00057595
BEGBATES : 265A-FL-280350-302-0012
DATE : 11/04/YEAR-1
FBIDESCR : MURRAY, JODY
FULLTEXT : FD-302 (Rev. 10-6-X)

FEDERAL BUREAU OF INVESTIGATION

Date of Transcription:
11/04/YEAR-1

JODY MURRAY, DOB 04/20/72 of Tampa, Florida was advised of the identity of the interviewing agent and the nature and purpose of the interview. Present for the interview was JOSH MURRAY, brother, and attorney TOMI BELL.

JODY MURRAY advised of the following:

JODY is Chief Executive Officer and Chairperson of the Board of Directors of the Citrus Florida Community Company (CFC). JODY has held this position for three years and has been employed with CFC for fifteen years.

In mid-YEAR-2, CFC began researching and pursuing a new orange juice additive that was supposed to make the orange juice last longer and taste better. This additive was called AOA and was projected to increase CFC's orange juice sales. DR. SAMI MYERS was in charge of that endeavor as the Head of the CFC Research Facility in Gulfport, Florida.

In mid-October, the Head of the Product Distribution Division, ASHLEY ALDEN, and MYERS were scheduled for a teleconference to discuss the final round of test results of the AOA additive. Also present at that teleconference were CHRIS SMART, Head of Marketing under ALDEN, and JESS HENLEY, head of Sales under ALDEN.

FEDERAL BUREAU OF INVESTIGATION

JODY was not at this meeting nor were they aware of what happened at the meeting. Suspicions arose when JODY did not receive the latest test results, but it was attributed to the furry surrounding preparations for the launch of AOA. After the launch, LYNN SMITH the head of Corporate Compliance and Human Resources initiated an investigation after a complaint by LOGAN WALTER, and employee working under SMART.

Although JODY was aware of the investigation, they were not informed of the specifics. JODY did receive an email from CORY CAMPBELL, CFC'S Corporate Counsel, stating that problems had arisen during the internal investigation of AOA but that they had been taken care of and there was no need to worry. This did not arouse any suspicions in JODY'S mind.

Months later JODY did award SMART, HENLEY, and ALDEN certificates for outstanding company work. They were not remotely related to the AOA additive but instead were issued in response to the Product Distribution department's significant increase in earnings of the last quarter. JODY also issued these certificates to all other members of the Product Distribution department.

Investigation on: **Citrus Florida Community Company Orange Juice Additive**

Location: **FBI Tampa Office** File Number: **M-INT-00057595**

By: **Agent Bernie Bentham** Date Dictated: **11/20/YEAR-1**

Attachment BB

[1]

FEDERAL BUREAU OF INVESTIGATION

Date of Transcription:
11/04/YEAR-1

LOGAN WALTER, DOB 1/17/90 of Tampa, Florida was advised of the identity of the interviewing agent and the nature and purpose of the interview. Also present at the interview was JO JONES, Assistant United State Attorney from the Middle District of Florida.

LOGAN WALTER advised of the following:

LOGAN is married with two children. Beginning in February of YEAR-1, LOGAN'S youngest daughter SARA was diagnosed with a severe form of asthma. At this time LOGAN had been employed with the Citrus Florida Community Company for almost ten years. LOGAN worked
as a member of the Marketing Team under CHRIS SMART.

On October 12, YEAR-2 LOGAN was headed back from lunch when they stopped outside of the conference room where ASHLEY ALDEN, CHRIS SMART, and JESS HENLEY were conducting a teleconference with DR. SAMI MYERS. The topic of the AOA additive peaked LOGAN'S interest so they lingered in the hallway instead of going back to their desk.

During this conversation, LOGAN overheard ALDEN state that the whole project was a waste of time and that people were going to be angry when they learned that nothing came out of the AOA project. ALDEN then went on to say that MYERS should destroy the

FEDERAL BUREAU OF INVESTIGATION

test results and go ahead with the launch and tell everyone the product works great. ALDEN later went on to state that they had significant stock options that were about to vest and the announcement that AOA did not work would kill the stock price before ALDEN could sell their shares.

After ALDEN, SMART, and HENLEY hang up with MYERS, ALDEN asked if they were all in agreement. HENLEY then said that they would do whatever ALDEN said because ALDEN was the boss. LOGAN then returned to their desk.

In March of YEAR-1, LOGAN spoke with LYNN SMITH, the Head of Corporate Compliance and Human Resources. At that meeting, LOGAN recounts everything heard during the teleconference. During the interview SMITH took extensive notes and impressions on LOGAN'S story. Five months later in September, LOGAN received a notice of termination.

Convinced that this firing is because of LOGAN'S report to human resources about ALDEN'S conversation, LOGAN filed a civil complaint.

Investigation on: **Citrus Florida Community Company Orange Juice Additive**

Location: **FBI Tampa Office** File Number: **M-INT-00057595**

By: **Agent Bernie Bentham** Date Dictated: **11/20/YEAR-1**

BEGPROONO : M-INT-00057595
BEGBATES : 265A-FL-280350-302-0031
DATE : 11/11/YEAR-1
FBIDESCR : TATE, JAMIE
FULLTEXT : FD-302 (Rev. 10-6-X)

[1]

FEDERAL BUREAU OF INVESTIGATION

Date of Transcription:
11/11/YEAR-1

JAMIE TATE, DOB 11/22/91 of Tampa, Florida was advised of the identity of the interviewing agent and the nature and purpose of the interview.

JAMIE TATE advised of the following:

JAMIE is an employee of the Citrus Florida Community Company and has been working there for the past eight years. After originally working in the production division of the household cleaner department at CFC, JAMIE was promoted to the sales team. As a member of the sales team, JAMIE works directly under JESS
HENLEY, Head of the Sales Team.

JAMIE was involved in the AOA additive product roll out in YEAR-2. The AOA additive was believed to make orange juice last longer and taste better. The Head of Product Distribution, ASHLEY ALDEN, was obsessed with the additive. They claimed it was the ticket to retirement. ALDEN constantly talked about the additive. HENLEY and CHRIS SMART were part of ALDEN'S inner circle. They were always meeting, most likely about AOA.

AOA was launched in late October of YEAR-2. Around that time, HENLEY seemed to be upset about something. It could have been the stress over the launch of AOA or something else. In addition to their mood change, JAMIE overheard HENLEY and SMART

FEDERAL BUREAU OF INVESTIGATION

fighting in the hallway just before the launch. They were fighting over some testing mess but JAMIE was unsure what they were talking about. Even during the AOA launch, HENLEY seemed very uneasy and agitated.

JAMIE and other members of the product distribution team were present. In addition to CFC employees, ALDEN invited the press to the launch and had the stage decorated with a banner and boxes of the new AOA orange juice. ALDEN stated that the additive was a wild success and the results of testing were good; so good, in fact, that the juice was flying off the shelves.

In the month or two following the launch there was a big push in the sales team to sell the AOA orange juice. But, two months after the launch, the product was pulled due to some profitability issue. JAMIE heard rumors that LYNN SMITH was investigating something about AOA but was never approached for an interview. JAMIE did speak with Attorney TOMI BELL about this issue several days ago. BELL is outside counsel representing CFC in this pending investigation.

Investigation on: **Citrus Florida Community Company Orange Juice Additive**

Location: **FBI Tampa Office** File Number: **M-INT-00057595**

By: **Agent Bernie Bentham** Date Dictated: **11/20/YEAR-1**

BEGPROONO : M-INT-00057595
BEGBATES : 265A-FL-280350-302-0034
DATE : 11/11/YEAR-1
FBIDESCR : SMART, CHRIS
FULLTEXT : FD-302 (Rev. 10-6-X)

[1]

FEDERAL BUREAU OF INVESTIGATION

Date of Transcription:
11/11/YEAR-1

CORY CAMPBELL, DOB 3/1/70 of Tampa, Florida was advised of the identity of the interviewing agent and the nature and purpose of the interview. Also present at the interview was CORY'S attorney TIM BRADY.

CORY CAMPBELL advised of the following:

CORY is the Citrus Florida Community Company's Corporate Counsel. CORY has been serving in that position for sixteen years. CORY graduated first in their class from a top five Law School and clerked for a United States Supreme Court justice upon graduation. CORY was an editor on the Law Review. After the clerkship Cory worked for two years at a top New York law firm handling complex commercial litigation. CORY did not enjoy the long hours and left to take an in-house position at CFC.

CORY received an investigative file from LYNN SMITH, Head of Corporate Compliance and Human Resources. The file contained information about the AOA additive that was recently launched by the Product Division Team. After receiving the file, CORY reviewed the file but determined that no additional investigation was merited. CORY then instructed SMITH to reprimand the employees involved but not to pursue anything further. This decision was based on the fact that the AOA additive was not profitable for the company and it was pulled two months after it was launched. Once CORY received the file

FEDERAL BUREAU OF INVESTIGATION

back from SMITH, it was placed with other confidential legal materials.

After finishing the investigation and closing the AOA matter, CORY sent an email to CFC'S Chief Executive Officer, JODY MURRAY. This email informed MURRAY that problems arose during the AOA investigation but they were resolved.

Upon being asked about the location of the test results of the AOA additive, CORY'S attorney advised him against answering. Following this advice, CORY refused to answer any questions relating to the test results and immediately terminated the interview. No follow-up interview was scheduled.

Investigation on: **Citrus Florida Community Company Orange Juice Additive**

Location: **FBI Tampa Office** File Number: **M-INT-00057595**

By: **Agent Bernie Bentham** Date Dictated: **11/20/YEAR-1**

[3]

FEDERAL BUREAU OF INVESTIGATION

Date of Transcription: 11/11/YEAR-1

CHRIS SMART, DOB 5/13/86 of Tampa, Florida was advised of the identity of the interviewing agent and the nature and purpose of the interview.

CHRIS SMART advised of the following:

CHRIS is the head of the Citrus Florida Community Company Marketing Team, working under ASHLEY ALDEN. CHRIS oversees twenty employees and works in conjunction with JESS HENLEY, head of the Sales Team.

On October 12, YEAR-2, CHRIS was on a teleconference call with ALDEN, HENLEY, and DR. SAMI MYERS. The topic of discussion was research concerning the new AOA additive which was purported to make orange juice last longer and taste better. During this call, ALDEN, HENLEY, and CHRIS, learned that AOA was ineffective and the project must be scrapped. In response to this revelation, ALDEN became infuriated and told DR. MYERS to destroy the research. ALDEN was upset not only because they had significant stock options tied to the launch of the AOA additive, but because they had become obsessed with the project and had planned on riding its success into retirement.

CHRIS never saw the final test results that were the subject of discussion during the teleconference.

BEGPROONO : M-INT-00057595
BEGBATES : 265A-FL-280350-302-0034
DATE : 11/11/YEAR-1
FBIDESCR : SMART, CHRIS
FULLTEXT : FD-302 (Rev. 10-6-X)

FEDERAL BUREAU OF INVESTIGATION

LOGAN WALTER worked directly under CHRIS. CHRIS had given WALTER a "Below Expectations" rating on their last performance review because WALTER had been underperforming, coming in late to work, and making simple mistakes. In response to a hard freeze that severely crippled CFC's production, CHRIS decided to let WALTER go based on this pervious performance review.

Once the internal investigation, headed up by LYNN SMITH the head of Corporate Compliance and Human Resources, was completed, CHRIS received a letter of reprimand and had their bonus reduced by 10%. But, in April of YEAR-1 CHRIS was awarded a certificate of appreciation for outstanding company work from CEO JODY MURRAY.

CHRIS refused to answer questions about the sale of their stock in connection with the launch of AOA.

Investigation on: **Citrus Florida Community Company Orange Juice Additive**

Location: **FBI Tampa Office** File Number: **M-INT-00057595**

By: **Agent Bernie Bentham** Date Dictated: **11/20/YEAR-1**

BEGPROONO : M-INT-00057595
BEGBATES : 265A-FL-280350-302-0037
DATE : 11/12/YEAR-1
FBIDESCR : HENLEY, JESS
FULLTEXT : FD-302 (Rev. 10-6-X)

FEDERAL BUREAU OF INVESTIGATION

Date of Transcription:
11/12/YEAR-1

JESS HENLEY, DOB 1/30/87 of Tampa, Florida was advised of the identity of the interviewing agent and the nature and purpose of the interview.

JESS HENLEY advised of the following:

JESS is the head of the Sales Team at the Citrus Florida Community Company. As the head of the team, JESS answers directly to ASHLEY ALDEN, the head of the Product Distribution division. JESS supervises a team of twenty people and was directly involved with the launch of a new orange juice additive, AOA.

On October 12, YEAR-2, JESS was on a teleconference call with ALDEN, CHRIS SMART, and DR. SAMI MYERS. The four were discussing the new test results concerning the AOA additive. During this call, ALDEN, SMART, and JESS, learned that the test results were negative, that AOA did not work, and the project must be scrapped. ALDEN became mad and angry when DR. MYERS gave them the news. ALDEN turned bright red like they were about to burst out in anger. ALDEN told DR. MYERS to destroy the test results and to go ahead with the launch of the product. There had been a lot of time, effort, and money put into the launch of AOA.

Afraid of being fired or being reprimanded, JESS agreed to go along with ALDEN'S decision. Everyone did what ALDEN said or they had to find another job. Even after the launch of the AOA product, JESS decided to not sell any stocks; mainly because of reservations about ALDEN'S orders. All JESS was worried about was losing their job.

Once the AOA orange juice was removed off the market only two months after its launch, JESS received a letter of reprimand and had their bonus reduced by 10%. JESS also complied with the internal investigation completed by the head of Corporate Compliance and Human Resources, LYNN SMITH.

BEGPROONO : M-INT-00057595
BEGBATES : 265A-FL-280350-302-0038
DATE : 11/12/YEAR-1
FBIDESCR : SMITH, LYNN
FULLTEXT : FD-302 (Rev. 10-6-X)

[1]

FEDERAL BUREAU OF INVESTIGATION

Date of Transcription: 11/12/YEAR-1

LYNN SMITH, DOB 12/28/81 of Tampa, Florida was advised of the identity of the interviewing agent and the nature and purpose of the interview.

LYNN SMITH advised of the following:

LYNN has been the head of Corporate Compliance and Human Resources at the Citrus Florida Community Company for the past eleven years. Prior to being promoted to head of the department, LYNN worked as a compliance officer in human resources. LYNN has both a bachelors and masters degree in psychology from State University.

In March of YEAR-1, LYNN was visited by LOGAN WALTER, an employee who was just recently fired. WALTER recounted a conversation overheard between DR. SAMI MYERS, CHRIS SMART, JESS HENLEY, and ASHLEY ALDEN. While standing outside the conference room door, WALTER heard the entire conversation about the new AOA additive.

The AOA additive was CFC's newest endeavor to increase profits. It was supposed to make orange juice last longer and taste better. ALDEN was the head of this initiative, with HENLEY and SMART working under them as heads of Sales and Marketing respectively. ALDEN was fully invested in the AOA additive; essentially staking their retirement on its success.

The conversation WALTER overheard occurred on October 12, YEAR-2 at the CFC headquarters in Tampa, Florida. ALDEN, SMART, and HENLEY were on the phone with someone who informed them that the AOA additive did not work. ALDEN then flipped out and began yelling at the person on the phone. ALDEN then told the person on the telephone to destroy the test results and pretend the product worked. SMART agreed to help ALDEN right away, but HENLEY was hesitant.

When asked why WALTER was bringing the information forward, they stated that they were afraid of being punished in retaliation. Upon receiving this information, LYNN began an internal investigation. During this investigation LYNN spoke with: WALTER, ALDEN, SMART, HENLEY, and DR. MYERS.

ALDEN stated that they planned on retiring off of the success of AOA and claimed that the only reason they told DR. MYERS to destroy the test was for the good of the company and because it was a good product. Although ALDEN couldn't remember exactly what was said but they remember being furious.

LYNN then interviewed SMART. SMART believed AOA was a brilliant marketing idea and was sorry that it was not more profitable for CFC. The early results were positive and so the only option was to go ahead with the launch. At the

FEDERAL BUREAU OF INVESTIGATION

teleconference ALDEN had a temper and got mad at DR. MYERS. ALDEN told DR. MYERS to get rid of the new numbers and rely on the preliminary test results. DR. MYERS seemed reluctant to agree, but decided to go along with the plan because the company needed the product, it was ready to go, and people expected it
to happen.

During the interview with HENLEY, they looked very uncomfortable. When told about what the internal investigation was regarding, HENLEY claimed it was all ALDEN'S idea. At the teleconference, ALDEN got mad and turned bright red when DR. MYERS told ALDEN the information. HENLEY decided to go along with ALDEN'S plan because HENLEY feared for their job.

Lastly, LYNN interviewed DR. MYERS. DR. MYERS told LYNN that they knew the AOA issue would come back to haunt them because it was a bad idea. The final test numbers showed that the product was ineffective. DR. MYERS told ALDEN, HENLEY, and SMART this during their teleconference. ALDEN became enraged, started yelling, and told DR. MYERS to destroy the test results. But, DR. MYERS did not follow this order; DR. MYERS still has the only remaining copy of the final test results. These results were given to LYNN. LYNN then placed the results in the corporate compliance investigation file.

After conducting all of the interviews, LYNN put together a file containing the interview notes and documents collected,

FEDERAL BUREAU OF INVESTIGATION

including the final test results. LYNN then took the file to the office of CFC General Counsel, CORY CAMPBELL. CAMPBELL reviewed the file then told LYNN to reprimand the employees in writing but to take no further action. ALDEN, HENLEY, and SMART all received written letters of reprimand and a decrease in their bonus of 10%.

LYNN then informed WALTER, the initial complaining employee, that the matter was closed and all appropriate action was taken. LYNN did not tell WALTER about what was found during the investigation or what punishment was given. Once the matter was finally closed, LYNN sent the investigation file back to CAMPBELL to store it with the other legal documents.

Investigation on: **Citrus Florida Community Company Orange Juice Additive**

Location: **FBI Tampa Office** File Number: **M-INT-00057595**

By: **Agent Bernie Bentham** Date Dictated: **11/20/YEAR-1**

BEGPROONO : M-INT-00057595
BEGBATES : 265A-FL-280350-302-0040
DATE : 11/13/YEAR-1
FBIDESCR : MYERS, DR. SAMI
FULLTEXT : FD-302 (Rev. 10-6-X)

FEDERAL BUREAU OF INVESTIGATION

Date of Transcription:
11/13/YEAR-1

DR. SAMI MYERS, DOB 09/11/75 of Gulfport, Florida was advised of the identity of the interviewing agent and the nature and purpose of the interview. Also present was DR. MYERS'S attorney, DAKOTA HOLT.

DR. MYERS advised of the following:

DR. MYERS also has two children, a son about to go off to college and a younger daughter. DR. MYERS is the head of the Citrus Florida Community Company's Research Facility located in Gulfport, Florida. DR. MYERS operates under the direction of the chief operating officer, KIM VANGUARD and has had over twenty-one years of experience working in the citrus industry.

CFC was conducting research into a new orange juice additive, AOA, that was supposed to make the juice taste better and last longer. Initial testing of AOA, done by DR. MYERS, looked very positive and suggested that the new line of AOA products could hit the shelves in a month. These results were then broadcast to investors and analysts by ASHLEY ALDEN, Head of CFC's Produce Distribution Department.

During the second round of testing, DR. MYERS determined that AOA was really ineffective and it would be best if the entire project were scrapped. DR. MYERS had a scheduled

FEDERAL BUREAU OF INVESTIGATION

teleconference with ALDEN, JESS HENLEY, and CHRIS SMART to discuss the results. Once DR. MYERS informed the trio about the negative results, ALDEN became angry and started yelling into the phone. ALDEN then told DR. MYERS that the test results must be destroyed and that CFC would be going ahead with the launch using the preliminary data. In response DR. MYERS pressed that the product really does not work and ALDEN was suggesting lying to consumers, the company, and investors. ALDEN then stated that they would not see the market tank CFC before there was a chance to sell their shares.

DR. MYERS did sell $55,000 in stock after the teleconference. However, DR. MYERS maintains that it was because their eldest child was going off to college and the $25,000 profit from the sale was needed to pay for the tuition.

Instead of destroying the test results, DR. MYERS secretly keeps a copy in their office. Once LYNN SMITH starts an internal investigation, DR. MYERS submits to an interview and hands over the results so that they can be placed in the file. After SMITH concluded the investigation, DR. MYERS received a written letter of reprimand and had their bonus reduced 10%.

Investigation on: **Citrus Florida Community Company Orange Juice Additive**

Location: **FBI Tampa Office**
By: **Agent Bernie Bentham**

File Number: **M-INT-00057595**
Date Dictated: **11/20/YEAR-1**

FEDERAL BUREAU OF INVESTIGATION

Date of Transcription: 11/13/15

ASHLEY ALDEN, DOB 10/20/78 of Tampa, Florida was advised of the identity of the interviewing agent and the nature and purpose of the interview.

ASHLEY ALDEN advised of the following:

ASHLEY is the head of the Product Distribution Division of the Citrus Florida Community Company. In that position, ASHLEY oversees the work of both the Marketing Team, headed up by CHRIS SMART, and the Sales Team, headed up by JESS HENLEY. ASHLEY has been serving in this position for the past four years and was previously with another orange juice company located in South Florida.

As the head of the distribution division, ASHLEY was tasked with overseeing the development and launch of a new orange juice additive called AOA. The initial research into AOA was promising and showed that the additive would indeed make orange juice taste better and last longer. This initial research was completed by the Head of the Research Facility, DR. SAMI MYERS.

The CEO of CFC, JODY MURRAY, was constantly in touch with ASHLEY regarding this new product. Most of this stemmed from the pressure MURRAY was under from investors to increase sales. Other local orange juice companies had been reducing their

FEDERAL BUREAU OF INVESTIGATION

product cost and cutting into profits. MURRAY essentially gave ASHLEY an ultimatum, increase sales by the end of the year or get fired.

The AOA additive was poised to be a huge success. But, secondary testing showed that AOA really did not work. ASHLEY first learned of this while on a teleconference with DR. MYERS, HENLEY, and SMART. When told of these results, ASHLEY was taken aback. ASHLEY asked DR. MYERS if they were sure about the results because CFC had already ordered new containers for the AOA juice and had a press conference set for the launch. Essentially, the whole project was a waste. While on this call, SMART and HENLEY told DR. MYERS to forget about the test results and to get rid of them. Someone even mentioned something about using a specific shredder to ensure that the results would be unrecognizable. There was an agreement that the launch should go on as planned, although ASHLEY does not remember any specifics. ASHLEY felt confident that AOA would actually work and that there were issues with the secondary testing so no harm would be done in pressing forward.

Two months after the launch, however, the product was discontinued. Contrary to initial projections, the AOA juice showed no profitability. But, someone that worked in ASHLEY'S division did come forward to the Head of Corporate Compliance and Human Resources, LYNN SMITH, and complained about what was heard during the conference call. ASHLEY does not know the identity of this employee but did submit to questioning from SMITH. ASHLEY does not know what became of the test results or what was contained in the investigation file.

After the internal investigation was completed, ASHLEY was given a letter of reprimand and had their bonus reduced by 10% that year.

IN THE UNITED STATES DISTRICT COURT
FOR THE MIDDLE DISTRICT OF FLORIDA
TAMPA DIVISION

UNITED STATES OF AMERICA,

Plaintiff

v. Case No.

ASHLEY ALDEN,

Defendant,

PLEA AGREEMENT

Pursuant to Rule 11(c) (1) (C,) of the Federal Rules of Criminal Procedure, the United States Department of Justice by the United States Attorney's for the Middle District of Florida ("the Department") and Ashley Alden ("the Defendant") agree to the following:

1. Defendant will plead guilty to Count 1 of the superseding Indictment, charging them with securities fraud in violation of Title 18, United States Code, Section 1348. Defendant agrees that they are pleading guilty because they guilty, and the facts contained in Exhibit A (attached and incorporated herein) are true and supply a factual basis for their plea. At the time the offenses were committed by the Defendant, the offense of security fraud as defined by Title 18, United States Code, Section 1348, carried the following statutory penalty:

    a. Maximum term of imprisonment: 25 years
    (Title 18 U.S.C §1348)
    b. Minimum term of imprisonment: 0 years
    (Title 18 U.S.C. § 1348)
    c. Maximum supervised release term: 5 years, to follow any term of imprisonment; if a condition of release is violated, Defendant may be sentenced to up to 2 years without credit for pre-release imprisonment or time previously served on post release supervision. (18 U.S.C § 3583 (b) & (e))
    d. Maximum fine: $250,000 or twice the gain/loss
    (18 U.S.C. § 3571 (b)(3) & (d)

Attachment CC

e. Restitution: as determined by the court pursuant to statute.
(18 U.S.C. § 3663)

f. Special Assessment: $100
(18 U.S.C. § 3013)

Sentencing Guidelines

2. The Defendant understands that, in imposing the sentence, the Court will be guided by the United States Sentencing Guidelines ("the Guidelines"). The Defendant understands that the Guidelines are advisory, not mandatory, but that the Court must consider the Guidelines in determining a reasonable sentence. The Defendant understands that their sentence is within the discretion of the sentencing judge.

3. Pursuant to Rule 11(c) (1) (C) of the Federal Rules of Criminal Procedure, the Defendant and the Department agree to ask the Court to impose a sentence of 24 months incarceration and to order forfeiture in the amount of $75,000.00. The Defendant agrees that they will not seek a sentence below 24 months incarceration.

4. The parties further agree that the Defendant's forfeiture of $75,000.00 in criminal proceeds fully satisfies the forfeiture, fine, and restitution provisions of the sentencing laws and guidelines.

Waiver of Rights

5. The Defendant, Ashley Alden, understands and acknowledges that by pleading guilty to one (1) count securities fraud pursuant to Title 18, United States Code, Section 1348, the Defendant hereby gives up the following rights as part of this agreement:

a) The right to plead not guilty to any criminal charges brought against them.

b) The right to a speedy and public trial by jury.

c) The right to the assistance of legal counsel at trial.

d) The right to confront and cross-examine witnesses against the Defendant.

e) The right to testify or to remain silent at trial.

f) The right to present evidence in opposition to the offense charged, including calling witnesses and subpoenaing witnesses to testify.

g) The right to be presumed innocent and to have the burden of proof placed on the government to prove each essential element of the charged offense beyond a reasonable doubt.

h) The right to pursue any affirmative defenses, Fourth Amendment or Fifth Amendment constitutional challenges, and other pretrial motions that have been filed, or may be filed in this Court.

i) Any right to appeal the imposition of the sentence against them.

j) The right to any defenses based on statute of limitations.

k) The right to any defenses based on improper jurisdiction.

6. The Defendant agrees not to appeal or collaterally attack the sentence (with the exception of claims for ineffective assistance of counsel), unless the Court imposes a term of imprisonment greater than 24 months.

Cooperation

7. The Defendant, Ashley Alden, agrees to cooperate fully with the Department, and any other government body or agency, by providing accurate, complete and truthful information regarding the Defendant's knowledge of any and all criminal activity, whether undertaken by the Defendant or others, in any way involving or related to the AOA additive scheme described within this plea agreement. The Defendant agrees to provide the Department, with all documents and evidence within the Defendant's possession, or whose whereabouts are known to the Defendant, related to this criminal investigation. It is an expressed condition of this agreement that the Defendant must, at all times, give accurate, complete, and truthful information and testimony. The Defendant may not withhold information from the government or refuse to testify truthfully and completely. The Defendant must attend all meetings, interviews, court appearances, and must timely provide all requested documents and records.

Defendant's Additional Obligations

8. Defendant agrees not to accept remuneration or compensation of any kind, directly or indirectly, for the dissemination through books, articles, speeches, interviews or any other means, of information regarding their work at Citrus Florida Community Company, or the prosecution of any civil or criminal cases against them.

9. Defendant agrees to pay the special assessment of $100.00 by check payable to the Clerk of the Court at or before sentencing. (18 U.S.C 3013 (a)(2)(a)).

10. Defendant agrees to forfeit to the government $75,000.00 to be satisfied by funds located within the StillStanding National Bank acct 1234567 which contains sufficient funds for this purpose and which constitutes proceeds of the offense to which the Defendant will plead guilty pursuant to this plea agreement. Defendant warrants that they are the sole owner of the property listed above, and they agree to hold the United States, its agents and employees harmless from any claims whatsoever in connection with the seizure or forfeiture of property covered by this agreement. Defendant further agrees to waive all interest in the amount listed above for forfeiture in any administrative or judicial forfeiture proceeding, whether criminal, civil, state or federal. Defendant agrees to consent to the entry of orders of forfeiture for such property and waives the requirements of Federal Rules of Criminal Procedure 32.2 and 43(a) regarding notice of forfeiture in the charging instrument, announcement of the forfeiture at sentencing and incorporation of the forfeiture in the judgment. Defendant acknowledges that they understand that the forfeiture of assets is part of the sentence that may be imposed in this case and waives any failure by the court to advise them of this, pursuant to Rule 11(b)(1)(J), at the time the guilty plea is accepted. Defendant further agrees to waive all constitutional and statutory challenges in any manner (including direct appeal, habeas corpus, or any other means with the exception of the right to allege ineffective assistance of counsel) to any forfeiture carried out in accordance with this agreement on any grounds, including that the forfeiture constitutes an excessive fine or punishment. Defendant agrees to take all steps to pass clear title to the forfeitable assets to the United States, and to testify truthfully in any related judicial proceeding. Defendant agrees not to seek a refund from the United States treasury of the amount of any taxes they paid in connection with the receipt of the $75,000 in proceeds from the offense to which they will plead guilty, and waives their right, title and interest to the taxes paid on that amount.

The Department's Obligations

11. The Department agrees that, except as provided for in this agreement, no criminal charges will be brought against the Defendant for any act or offense in which they engaged in their capacity as an Employee of CFC Corp., or arising out of such employment, and the Department will move after sentencing to dismiss the remaining counts of the Superseding Indictment against Defendant with prejudice.

Scope

12. This agreement does not bind any federal, state or local prosecuting authority other than the Department, and does not prohibit the Department, or any other department, agency or commission of the United States from initiating or prosecuting any civil, administrative or

tax proceedings directly or indirectly involving the Defendant.

Complete Agreement

13. No promises, agreements or conditions have been entered into by the parties other than those set forth in this Agreement and none will be entered into unless memorialized in writing and signed by all parties. This Agreement supersedes any prior promises, agreements, or conditions between the parties, including any written proffer agreements. To become effective, this agreement must be signed by all signatories listed below.

Dated: Tampa Florida
March 20, YEAR-0

Jo Jones
Assistant United States Attorney

Jo Jones

Ashley Alden

Ashley Alden

Attachment CC

IN THE UNITED STATES DISTRICT COURT
FOR THE MIDDLE DISTRICT OF FLORIDA
TAMPA DIVISION

UNITED STATES OF AMERICA,

Plaintiff,

v. Case No.

ASHLEY ALDEN,

Defendant,

Exhibit A to Plea Agreement

The following factual statement made by the Defendant Ashley Alden is submitted to provide a factual basis for my plea of guilty to Count 1 (securities fraud) of the above captioned Superseding Indictment, charging me with securities fraud in violation of Title 18, United States Code, Section 1348.

I was the Head of Product Distribution of Citrus Florida Community Company (CFC) during the fall of YEAR-2. While in that position, I and other employees of CFC misled investors, purchasers, and the public about the effectiveness of the orange juice additive "AOA" that was being marketed by CFC, to preserve and to increase the value of CFC stock and of stock options held by myself and other employees.

I, along with other CFC employees, upon hearing of negative final test results on the effectiveness of the orange juice additive AOA, during a conference call on Oct. 12, YEAR-2, ordered the suppression of the test results which showed that AOA was ineffective. Further, I and the other employees referred only to earlier positive test results when talking to customers and purchasers of CFC orange juice products, after the suppression of the final test results.

Attachment CC

On Oct. 26, YEAR-2, I announced at a press conference, that the final test results on AOA were positive, and that they showed AOA to be an effective additive. The stock market recorded a gain of $6 per share of CFC later that day.

On Oct. 27, YEAR-2, I sold stock options totaling $450,000.00. My share of the sales amounted to $275,000.00.

I understood that my conduct would have a material effect on the value of CFC stock, and that investors and purchasers alike would rely on the deception so perpetrated. CFC stock is traded on the New York Stock Exchange. I also understood that interstate wire transmissions including email, telephone, and satellite transmissions would be used to transmit the deceptive information that I and other employees released.

The preceding is a summary of facts for the purpose of providing the Court with a factual basis for my guilty plea to the Indictment. It does not include all the facts known to me concerning criminal activity in which I and other employees of CFC engaged. I make this statement knowingly and voluntarily.

Ashley Alden

Ashley Alden
Defendant

March 20, YEAR-0

Attachment CC

Grand Jury Testimony of Lee Laser

AUSA: My name is Jo Jones, and I am an Assistant United States Attorney for the Middle District of Florida. We appreciate your being with us here today, Professor. Can you state your name and tell us about your background?

LASER: I am Lee Laser and I am a professor at State University where I teach chemistry and have taught there for the last ten years. I graduated from Tech College with a BS degree in chemistry and went onto Prestigious University where I received both my masters and Phd. My specialty is analytical chemistry. I presently hold an endowed chair titled the Juicet Professor of Analytical Chemistry. It's named after Carl Juicet, the owner of Grove Distributers - a major distributor of citrus products. Juicet gave State University one million dollars and I was selected to hold this chair based upon a competitive process.

AUSA: Professor Laser, did you have an opportunity to analyze the contents of orange juice produced by CFC during the period in which CFC was claiming that the orange juice produced by their company had a longer shelf life than other juices?

LASER: I sure did. I was fascinated when I saw this label on the juice and I decided that it would make a wonderful project for my graduate students to analyze the contents. Basically they were asked to reverse engineer this product to see if they could determine the contents and replicate what was there.

AUSA: What did you find out in doing this?

LASER: In reading the student papers it was clear that CFC was scamming folks. There was absolutely no difference from the regular OJ and this supposedly new OJ. The only difference was the label that said this product could last longer on your shelf. All five of my graduate students came up with the exact same result.

AUSA: Are you saying that there was absolutely no difference whatsoever?

LASER: You got it. These folks were marketing a fraud.

AUSA: Thank you, Professor Laser.

Attachment DD

Report for Jody Murray, Cory Campbell, Sami Myers, Jess Henley, Ashley Alden, and Chris Smart on CFC Investigation of AOA

Dear Interested Parties:

I was asked to provide you with a report that analyzed an additive used in orange juice at CFC during approximately a two month time frame from October to December of YEAR-2. I conducted specific chemical analysis tests on this product including doing reverse engineering. I also reviewed the data of Dr. Sami Myers in reaching my two conclusions. First, it is my opinion that Dr. Myers incorrectly performed one of the tests they conducted concerning the AOA. Second, however, it is my opinion that if these tests had been performed correctly they would have discovered a monumental find in prolonging the longevity of orange juice.

Oranges are a fruit from citrus x sinensis, a tree grown in relatively warm climates like Florida. Although it originated in Asia, it is widely grown here in the United States. Although there are a host of different oranges available, for purposes of my testing I limited myself to that used by CFC in their production of orange juice.

In order to analyze the consistency in the juice produced from these oranges it was necessary to conduct a multitude of different tests. One needs to perform both qualitative and quantitative analysis. Additionally, one should never limit quantitative analysis to one specific form of test, such as a flame test, chemical test, or volumetric analysis. To ascertain proper results, it is important to look at a multitude of different tests. Some will stop with just a flame test because they lack state of the art instruments or funding to conduct additional tests. But it is important that these additional tests be used because flame tests do not extract all ingredients, especially when one is not dealing with carbons.

Thus, I conducted gravimetric analysis that weighs the substance before and after, volumetric analysis, microscopy, and separation. Each of these tests provided confirmation that this additive existed in the CFC product that was marked as providing a longer shelf life, specifically the product sold by CFC during the latter portion of YEAR-2. I also conducted a flame test, which as I expected failed to produce any results.

I also had the opportunity to examine the work product of Dr. Sami Myers. First let me say that Dr. Sami Myers is highly respected in scientific circles having graduated from Cal Tech, where I am presently a professor. Dr. Myers graduated first in their class, winning the award for being the most innovative student and most likely to succeed. I personally had the pleasure of having Dr. Sami Myers in two of my chemistry classes and they were truly an incredible student. Dr. Sami Myers left Cal Tech years ago and I have had no contact with them during this time frame.

I reviewed the work of Dr. Sami Myers and it was clear that the initial tests on the AOA product were progressing extremely well. Unfortunately, Dr. Myers appeared to rush on one set of tests and this failed to allow sufficient time for the product to fully mature. I do not know what pressures were being placed on Dr. Sami Myers to cause them to rush with this test. I can say that had this test moved slowly, it would have demonstrated that Dr. Sami Myers had discovered an additive that can prolong the shelf life of orange juice.

I have been an analytical chemist and professor at Cal Tech for over twenty-five years. I have written over one hundred articles and five books. I have testified in over fifty court cases as an expert in the field of chemical analysis. Of those fifty cases, two of them have been for the government and the rest have been cases where the defense hired me. My research has included extensive studies that I have performed on the longevity of liquids.

My hourly out-of-court rate is $300 an hour and my in-court rate is $ 500 an hour. I also charge for travel, telephone, fax, and supplies. In this case, my fee for this report is $25,000. Additional charges will be assessed should I be needed to testify at trial.

Very truly yours,

Amari Andersen

Amari Andersen
Andersen Professor of Analytical Chemistry
California Institute of Technology

Direct Examination of Lee Laser

AUSA: Can you state your name and spell your last name for the court reporter?

LASER: My name is Lee Laser. L - A- S- E-R.

PROSECUTOR: Professor Laser, where are you employed.

LASER: I am a professor at State University where I teach chemistry.

AUSA: How long have you been with State University?

LASER: It's been almost ten years, but I am now tenured.

AUSA: Tell us about your educational background?

LASER: I graduated from Tech College with a BS degree in chemistry and went onto Prestigious University where I received both my masters and Phd. My specialty is analytical chemistry.

AUSA: Are you presently a chaired professor at State University?

LASER: Yes, I hold the title of the Juicet Professor of Analytical Chemistry.

AUSA: What is analytical chemistry?

LASER: It's the study of separation, identification, and quantification of chemical components.

AUSA: Are there different methods of approaching analytical chemistry?

LASER: Yes, classical methods - sometimes called wet chemistry - use separations such as extraction or qualitative analysis to determine the components. Quantitative analysis on the other hand is achieved by measurement of weight or volume. There are also many different instruments that can be used. Some folks use chromaography, while others use electrophoresis.

AUSA: Have you written any articles related to analytical chemistry?

LASER: Yes, I have written over fifty articles in this area.

AUSA: Have you ever been qualified in court as an expert in the area of analytical chemistry?

LASER: Yes, I have testified three other times.

AUSA: At this time, your honor, we move for Dr. Laser to be held to be an expert in analytical chemistry.

THE COURT: Any objection.

DEFENSE COUNSEL: We have no objection, your honor.

AUSA: Professor Laser, did you have an opportunity to review the analysis conducted by Dr. Sami Myers?

LASER: I did.

AUSA: Can you tell us what you found?

LASER: It was clear that Dr. Myers had not followed basic scientific methods.

AUSA: Can you explain what basic scientific methods are?

LASER: Yes, one needs to first determine the question, then do background research, then construct a hypothesis. After constructing a hypothesis one needs to then test it via experimentation. One then analyzes the data and reaches a conclusion.

AUSA: Where exactly did Dr. Myers fail in the scientific method here?

LASER: It was clear that Dr. Myers failed to conduct sufficient testing to see if the product really would work.

AUSA: Professor Laser did you have an opportunity to analyze the components of the orange juice produced by CFC during the period in which CFC was claiming that the orange juice produced by their company had a longer shelf life than other juices?

LASER: Yes, I did. I reverse engineered this product.

AUSA: What tests did you run?

LASER: I performed a flame test. This basically tests to see the reactions from using a flame over the product.

AUSA: And what did you find?

LASER: Well as stated in the ten page report that I provided to your office, we found that there were no active ingredients that distinguished these two orange juices - the one with the label that said it had a longer life and the one without this label.

AUSA: Are you saying that there was absolutely no difference whatsoever?

LASER: That is correct.

AUSA: Thank you, Professor Laser.

Direct Examination of Ashley Alden

AUSA: Would you please state your name and spell your last name for the court reporter?

ALDEN: My name is Ashley Alden, that's A-L-D-E-N.

AUSA: Alden what was your association with CFC in YEAR-2?

ALDEN: I was the head of the product distribution division.

AUSA: How many employees worked directly for you?

ALDEN: 42.

AUSA: Who did you report to?

ALDEN: Kim Vanguard the Chief Operating Officer of CFC.

AUSA: And who did Vanguard report to?

ALDEN: Jody Murray, the CEO of the company.

AUSA: Did you personally have interaction with Murray?

ALDEN: Constantly. Murray would be in meetings, would send me emails, and would visit me in my office.

AUSA: Were you initially indicted for the crimes of honest services fraud, securities fraud, insider trading, and conspiracy?

ALDEN: Yes, I also had a charge of obstructing justice.

AUSA: Did you enter a plea to any of these charges?

ALDEN: Yes, I pleaded guilty to securities fraud.

AUSA: I now show you what has been marked as Governments Exhibit CC. Do you recognize it?

ALDEN: Yes, that's the plea agreement that I entered into.

AUSA: And is that your signature on the plea agreement?

ALDEN: Yes.

Attachment GG

AUSA: Did we promise you any favoritism at sentencing in return for this plea?

ALDEN: No.

AUSA: Does this plea require you to testify truthfully at this trial?

ALDEN: It does.

AUSA: Now let's talk about what happened back in October of YEAR-2?

ALDEN: OK.

AUSA: Do you remember a meeting on October 12, YEAR-2 to discuss the AOA additive?

ALDEN: It's a meeting I will never forget.

AUSA: Who was at that meeting?

ALDEN: It was Chris Smart, Jess Henley, and myself. During the meeting we called Dr. Sami Myers.

AUSA: Tell us what happened at the meeting.

ALDEN: I called Myers, who worked in Gulfport, to discuss the test results from the new additive to orange juice called AOA. Myers claimed that this AOA could make us a lot of money as it would prolong the shelf life of orange juice. Myers suddenly then says that it doesn't work. I have to say that I lost my temper for a minute. You see CEO Jody Murray had been on my back to increase sales. We had been feeling the pressure of local orange juice companies reducing their product cost and cutting into our profit. Murray said that I better come up with something before the end of the year, or I'd be history with the company. Quite frankly I wish Murray had just fired me. They are a jerk.

DEFENSE COUNSEL: Objection, your honor, improper characterization.

AUSA: I'll rephrase my question? So tell us about the telephone call with Dr. Sami Myers?

ALDEN: Anyway, I called Myers to find out why we still hadn't received the final test results. And that's when Myers said it didn't work. They just all of sudden said - the additive failed and the test results confirmed that it was a failure. I said -- what should we do? After all we already had ordered the new bottles, new labels, and we had announced it to the public. I said, "you mean to tell me this whole project is a waste of time. I've got people on the street expecting this thing to hit the shelves any time now. What do you think is going to happen if they find out we've got nothing." That's when Chris Smart and Jess Henley said - relax. They said we can do this. Smart said, "no one has to know what the test results said." Henley then said, "Myers and us are the only ones that know what happened and none of us talks." I was shocked then when Chris Smart speaks into the phone and tells Myers to shred the results. Smart even went so far to say - "be sure and use a criss-cross shredder so that no one will know the results."

AUSA: And what happened next?

ALDEN: Smart, Henley and Myers agreed that we would not let the test results leave the room. They said, let's go with it on the market and then we can quietly take it out in a couple of months. I was shocked, scared, and really bothered by what they were doing. I only wish I had come forward and stopped it then. But I am coming forward now and saying this lie has got to stop.

AUSA: Do you know if Jody Murray knew what happened with the AOA?

ALDEN: They had to have known. We always send the test results when we receive them and this time we didn't. It was obvious that something was being hidden. Why did they suddenly give each of us commendations for our work with the company?

AUSA: I now show you what has been marked as Government Exhibit T, can you identify it?

ALDEN: Yes, that's the commendations the three of us received in April YEAR-1. We also received huge bonuses that year. They took a bit away later on, but this was just to make it look like they were reprimanding us. It was only 10% of the huge bonuses that we received for the year. They knew what was going on.

AUSA: Thank you Alden, I have no further questions your Honor.

UNITED STATES DISTRICT COURT
MIDDLE DISTRICT OF FLORIDA
TAMPA DIVISION

UNITED STATES OF AMERICA

v. Case No. 8:11-cr-XXXX

JODY MURRAY
SAMI MYERS

GOVERNMENT
PROPOSED JURY INSTRUCTION

Willful Blindness

Members of the Jury:

To find the defendants Jody Murray and Sami Myers guilty of Wire Fraud under the Honest Services Provision, Securities Fraud, Insider Trading, Conspiracy, or Obstruction of Justice, you must find that the government proved beyond a reasonable doubt that the defendants knew that a crime was occurring. In this case, there is the question of whether the defendants knew that the orange juice additive did not work and acted upon that information, either to conceal it or profit upon it. When, as in this case, knowledge of a particular fact or circumstance is an essential part of the offense charged, the government may prove that the defendants knew of that fact or circumstance if the evidence proves beyond a reasonable doubt that the defendants closed their eyes to what would otherwise have been obvious to them.

No one can avoid responsibility for a crime by ignoring what is obvious. Thus, you may find that the defendants knew that the orange juice additive did not work based on evidence which proves that: (1) the defendants were aware of a high probability of this information, and (2) the defendants tried to avoid learning about this information.

As such, the knowledge component of the crimes will be satisfied, that is the defendants will have knowledge of the crime, if the defendants were indifferent to the circumstances around them.

UNITED STATES DISTRICT COURT
MIDDLE DISTRICT OF FLORIDA
TAMPA DIVISION

UNITED STATES OF AMERICA

v.

Case No. 8:11-cr-XXXX

JODY MURRAY,
SAMI MYERS

Defense
Willful Blindness

Members of the Jury:

To find the defendants Jody Murray and Sami Myers guilty of Wire Fraud under the Honest Services Provision, Securities Fraud, Insider Trading, Conspiracy, or Obstruction of Justice, you must find that the government proved beyond a reasonable doubt that the defendants knew that a crime was occurring. If a Defendant's knowledge of a fact is an essential element of a crime, you may find that such knowledge existed if you find that the Defendant maintained deliberate ignorance by deliberately and affirmatively avoiding knowledge of the fact—unless the defendant actually believed that the fact did not exist.

Thus, you may find that the defendants knew that the orange juice additive did not work based on evidence which proves that: (1) the defendant was aware of a high probability of this information, and (2) the defendants consciously and deliberately tried to avoid learning about this information.

You may not find that the defendants did not know that the orange juice additive did not work if you find that the defendants actually believed that it did work. Also, you may not find that the defendants knew that the additive did not work if you find only that the defendants should have known of this fact or that a reasonable person would have known of a high probability of the additive not working. It is not enough that the defendants may have been stupid or foolish, or may have acted out of inadvertence or accident. You must find that the defendants were actually aware of a high probability that the additive did not work and that the defendant deliberately took actions to avoid learning about it. Negligence, recklessness, foolishness, or carelessness is not enough to prove knowledge on the part of the defendant.

JURY INSTRUCTIONS

Honest Services

Defendants Sami Myers, Jess Henley, Ashley Alden, and Chris Smart are charged pursuant to Title 18, of the United States Code, Sections 1341 and 1346. Sections 1341 and 1346 make it a Federal crime or offense for anyone to use the mails or an interstate carrier in carrying out a scheme to fraudulently deprive another of an intangible right of honest services.

Defendants Sami Myers, Jess Henley, Ashley Alden, and Chris Smart are charged pursuant to 18 USC §§ 371, 1341, and 1346. Sections 371, 1341 and 1346, make it a Federal crime or offense for anyone to conspire to use the mails or an interstate carrier in carrying out a scheme to fraudulently deprive another of an intangible right of honest services.

Defendants Cory Campbell and Jody Murray are charged pursuant to 18 USC §§ 1343 and 1346. Sections 1343 and 1346, make it a Federal crime or offense for anyone to use interstate wire communications facilities in carrying out a scheme to fraudulently deprive another of an intangible right of honest services.

To "deprive another of the intangible right of honest services" is to violate, or to cause an employee or agent of another person to violate, the employee's or agent's duty to provide honest services to the employer.

With regard to employers in the private sector, the Government must prove that the employee intended to breach a fiduciary duty, and that the employee foresaw, or reasonably should have foreseen, that the employer might suffer an economic harm as a result of that breach.

Under the law, every agent or employee representing or working for someone else—the employer—has a duty (called a fiduciary duty) to act honestly and faithfully in all of their dealings with the employer, and to transact business in the best interest of the employer, including a duty to make full and fair disclosure to the employer of any personal interest or profit [or "kickback"] the employee expects to derive or has derived from any transaction in which they participate in the course of the employment.

A "kickback" includes any kind of undisclosed payment or reward to an employee for dealing in the course of employment with the person making the payment so that the employee's personal financial interest interferes with the employee's duty to secure the most favorable bargain for the employer.

It is not necessary that the Government prove all of the details alleged in the indictment concerning the precise nature and purpose of the scheme; or that the material transmitted by mails or wire was itself false or fraudulent; or that the alleged scheme actually succeeded in defrauding anyone; or that the use of interstate wire communications facilities was intended as the specific or exclusive means of accomplishing the alleged fraud; or that the Defendants personally used the wire communication facility.

Attachment JJ

What must be proved beyond a reasonable doubt is that the Defendants, with intent to defraud, knowingly and willfully devised, intended to devise, or participated in, a scheme to defraud substantially the same as the one alleged in the indictment by giving a bribe or accepting a kickback in connection with their position; and that the use of the mails, interstates carrier, or interstate wire communications facilities was closely related to the scheme because the Defendants either used, or caused to be used, wire communications facilities in interstate commerce in an attempt to execute or carry out the scheme.

Knowingly and Willfully

The Government has charged, in the indictment, that the Defendants "knowingly and willfully" committed fraud. The word "knowingly," as that term is used in the indictment or in these instructions, means that the act was done voluntarily and intentionally and not because of mistake or accident.

The word "willfully," as that term is used in the indictment or in these instructions, means that the act was committed voluntarily and purposely, with the specific intent to do something the law forbids; that is with bad purpose either to disobey or disregard the law. This requires the Government to prove beyond a reasonable doubt that the Defendants acted with a "specific intent to do something the law forbids; that is, with bad purpose and this must have been done voluntarily and intentionally. If the Government fails to prove this, their burden is not met and you must acquit the defendants.

Reasonable and Good Faith Defense

The good faith of a defendant is a complete defense to the charges of fraud contained in the indictment because good faith on the part of a defendant is, simply, inconsistent with the intent to defraud alleged in that charge.

A person who acts, or causes another person to act, on a belief or an opinion honestly held is not punishable under these statutes merely because the belief or opinion turns out to be inaccurate, incorrect, or wrong. An honest mistake in judgment or an error in management does not rise to the level of intent to defraud.

A defendant does not act in "good faith" if, even though they honestly hold a certain opinion or belief, that defendant also knowingly makes false or fraudulent pretenses, representations, or promises to others.

The mail and wire fraud statutes are written to subject to criminal punishment only those people who knowingly defraud or attempt to defraud.

While the term "good faith" has no precise definition, it means, among other things, a belief or opinion honestly held, an absence of malice or ill will, and an intention to avoid taking unfair advantage of another.

In determining whether or not the government has proven that the defendant acted with an intent to defraud or whether the defendant acted in good faith, the jury must consider all of the evidence in the case bearing on the defendant's state of mind.

The burden of proving good faith does not rest with the defendant because the defendant does not have any obligation to prove anything in this case. It is the government's burden to prove to you, beyond a reasonable doubt, that Defendant acted with the intent to defraud.

If the evidence in the case leaves the jury with a reasonable doubt as to whether the defendant acted with an intent to defraud or in good faith, the jury must acquit Defendant.

Attachment JJ